PARTICIPATORY GOVERNANCE IN THE CONTEXT OF SECESSION

PARTICIPATORY GOVERNANCE IN THE CONTEXT OF SECESSION

A Case Study of Bangladesh

Gargi Sengupta

KALPAZ

ISBN: 978-93-5128-032-3

Price: ₹ 465

First Published 2014

Published by

Kalpaz Publications
C-30, Satyawati Nagar,
Delhi - 110052
E-mail: kalpaz@hotmail.com Ph.: 9212142040

Laser Typesetting : Rajender Vashist, Delhi
Printed at: G. Print Process, Delhi

Cataloging in Publication Data--DK
Courtesy: D.K. Agencies (P) Ltd. <docinfo@dkagencies.com>

Sengupta, Gagri.

Participatory governance in the context of secession : a case study of Bangladesh / Gargi Sengupta.

p. cm.
Includes bibliographical references (p.) and index.
ISBN 9789351280323

1. Bangladesh--Politics and government--1971- 2. Political participation--Bangladesh. 3. Secession--Bangladesh. I. Title.

DDC 320.95492 23

Contents

Preface 7

Acknowledgements 9

List of Tables and Figures 11

Abbreviations 13

Introduction 15

1. **Issues Concerning: Political Right to Self-Determination, Secession and Participatory Governance** 25

   The Concept of Political Right to Self-determination and Secession • The Liberal Approach • The Genesis of the Concept of Secession • Self Determination, United Nations and Secession • Right to Secession is What Right? • The Marxist Approach • The Concept of Participatory Governance.

2. **The Breaking of Pakistan vis-a-vis the Making of Bangladesh: Bangladesh's Liberation War of 1971** 57

   History of Bengal After the Coming of British Rule to 1947 (Partition of India) • From the Formation of East Pakistan to the Birth of Bangladesh 1947 to 1971 • Factors Responsible for the Rise of Growing Disparities between East Pakistan and West Pakistan • Declaration of Independence of Bangladesh and the Role of India • The Idea of Humanitarian Assistance, the Role of UN and India in the Liberation War of Bangladesh.

3. Government and Governance of Bangladesh **97**

Governmental Transitions and Regime Change in Bangladesh: From Independence to the Present • Is the Governance System of Bangladesh Participatory in Nature? • Present Features of Bangladesh Governance • Governance in Bangladesh and the Issue of Human Development.

Conclusion 135

Bibliography 145

Index 151

Preface

Participatory governance allows people to exercise their voice and vote in the process of implementation, execution and evaluation of any policies. This is a kind of freedom as well as right which a person enjoys within a democratic society. In this book I primarily examine how people of a country is actually accepting and practicing these two options/opportunities.

This book is an outcome of my M.Phil dissertation submitted to University of Delhi. While I was writing my M.Phil dissertation my hypothesis was, if we have more participatory governance then the chance of secession gets reduced. This hypothesis was proved through the case study of Bangladesh (East Pakistan seceded from West Pakistan in 1971). For any country, maintaining its sovereignty is not only a political matter but it is more of matter of prestige, both nationally and internationally. Therefore if a group of people reject to accept the sovereignty of their present state and demand for a new sovereignty then it is a matter of shame for the parent state. So if the issue is so emotional and intense then why people want to secede?

Chapter 2 of this book discusses how the people of East Pakistan suffered at the hands of West Pakistan which resulted into the demand for secession and finally Pakistan broke and Bangladesh was formed in 1971. This book examines how this secession affects the people of Bangladesh? Are they safe and enjoying their social economic and political freedom in their own designed country. Chapter 3 of this book discusses the present scenario of Bangladesh politics and socio-economic life.

Today when we cherish that democratic governance should flourish and take roots then we must have participation and active involvement of the people otherwise democracy will remain "incomplete". Through this book I am basically trying to link two absolutely divergent concepts – Participatory Governance and Secession, which seem to be opposite but actually share a relationship.

Gargi Sengupta

Acknowledgements

I would like to convey my sincere gratitude to Prof. Achin Vanaik, my M.Phil supervisor who not only gave his valuable time and expertise to read and comment on my work at every stage but also has been a source of inspiration. His invaluable suggestions and guidance have helped me a lot. He has also led me to new dimensions and perspectives on the subject of study. Without his support, the study would not have been possible.

I am also thankful to the Department of Political Science, University of Delhi, Central Reference Library, Arts Library and Nehru Memorial Library for their help at various stages of my work.

I would like to thank my husband, parents, friends as well as well-wishers for their encouragement and motivation in completing this book.

Gargi Sengupta

List of Tables and Figures

Tables

2.1. Economic Growth Rate between East Pakistan and West Pakistan 67

2.2. Disparity Reason between East Pakistan and West Pakistan 68

Figures

2.1. The Birth of Bangladesh in 1971. 56

3.1. Political Map of Bangladesh 97

Abbreviations

AL	–	Awami League
BKSAL	–	Bangladesh Krishak Sramik Awami League
BNP	–	Bangladesh Nationalist Party
HDI	–	Human Development Index
HDR	–	Human Development Report
JRB	–	Jatio Rakkhi Bahini
RSDLP	–	Russian Social Democratic Labour Party
UNO	–	United Nations Organisations
UNDP	–	United Nations Development Programme

Introduction

In the book "*Political Liberalism*", John Rawls in an interesting paragraph wrote "a conception of political legitimacy is that in which the political power and authority is justified only if such authority is acceptable to all citizens bound by it". This particular kind of political liberalism, which is highlighted by John Rawls and other liberal philosophers, opened the idea of political freedom and liberty under the umbrella of justice. It is in this understanding of the concept of political freedom that terms like autonomy, self-determination and secession do not remain as just buzzwords. Rather they are key to defining the overall jurisdiction of a state. Although these terms share certain commonalities among themselves, yet they are not the same and cannot be used interchangeably. The reason behind this argument is that "autonomy" refers to a right of the people to have self-governance that is the ability or capacity of self-rule. But "self-determination" on the other hand is about the freedom of the people of a given territory enjoys to determine their own political status independent from their current state. Therefore, political self-determination is limited to its regional and territorial expressions.[1] The third term "secession" is one step ahead of both these processes. The term "Secession" has been described as a process of withdrawal of territory and its population from an existing state and the creation of a new state on that territory (with a new sovereign).[2]

Notwithstanding the fact that on a conceptual basis, these three terms are different but national groups (not all but many) have a tendency to interpret their right of self-governance as a right of self-determination first and then from this right of self-determination to a right for having a state of their own, i.e., a state which belongs to their people. This mixing of various terms makes the issue or situation more complex because the ultimate proposition which comes out of it is to have an "independent statehood". Therefore, many scholars are skeptical of this "interpretation of national self-determination as the right to independent statehood" because they believe that it leads to a "Balkanisation effect".[3] According to Brian Barry and David Miller, the national groups only have the right to claim an independent state. But usually it is observed that ethnic groups often adopt the posture of being a national-group for claiming the right to statehood to protect and preserve their own group claims. In the long run, this tendency gives rise to more division and more distinction.[4] Thus, the issue of "independent statehood" or "secession" becomes an important concern in the present.

Nationalism is a feeling, love, respect of a person towards his/her own nation, nationality and national culture. It is the concept of national culture, which highlights the idea of adherence of a person towards his own particular culture and that can ultimately lead to the demand for having one's own independent statehood. Therefore, the strong desire of a person for his/her history, culture, language, religion and so on can result into the breaking of a state and the making of a new state which we call as a process of "secession".

According to Amartya Sen, apart from history and background, there are a variety of categories existing to which a person can belong.[5] Therefore, belongingness to all the groups is important for a person. This belongingness to various categorical identities is centrally organised around ethnicity, religion, language, gender, etc. Because of this, fragmentation takes place in the society in terms of individual and collective identities. These identities can be characterised as overlapping, heterogeneous and multiple in nature. Such identities of different nature act as markers around which people design their identity. The positive effect of the categorical identities is that it gives more recognition to specificities and particularities. But the negative effect of this recognition is that people can easily be moulded in the name of these identities, and moreover it makes people conscious about their self-interest. This may result in the identity of ethnicity, religion or race becoming the basis for the emergence of a nationalism that could demand an independent sovereign state.

Coming again to the issue of nationalism, it can be said that the concept of nationalism has the following two different meanings:[6]

(1) The attitude of the people of a nation towards their national identity.

(2) The action that the people of a nation take when they seek to achieve self-determination.

Among these two perceptions, the first one is well-accepted as it is not complex, because every member of a nation cares or feels about his/her nation as it gives every member a sense of belongingness to a particular nation. But on the other hand, the second perception creates greater complications. It involves the issue of full-statehood. The problem does not lie in the demand of self-determination. The problem comes when this demand changes into the demand for having an independent statehood (right to secession). One of the forms of achieving this independent statehood apart from political agreement is secession (which is the central issue that I will explore throughout my work).

In the period of 1989–1990, the world had witnessed two types of changes. One was on the political front and the other was on the economic front. After the disintegration of the USSR and the break-up of the Berlin Wall, the world witnessed the tremendous rise of secessionist movements. It is because of the detachment of territories from the sovereign jurisdiction of the earlier states. This break-up has become a fundamental way of gaining independence.[7] This development was at the political level. While on the economic front, the world witnessed the coming of an integrated economic process called globalisation. It is the name of that process in which the world's economy gets integrated through free flow of capital, labour, goods and services. This highly integrated world believes in the concept of inter-connectedness and interdependency on one side and dissolution of territorial borders or barriers on the other side.[8] Here the important point of concern is that how to manage the cause and effect of both these processes on each other because they came at a one common point of time. One believes in the increasing recognition of the power and significance of independent sovereign states and the second process supported the decrease of power and significance of sovereign states. According to Aleksandar Pavkovic and Peter Radan, despite this globalisation process, the demand for independent statehood has continued unabated. Because of global spread of new communication technologies, internet-accessibilities, etc.,[9] the capacity of secessionist mobilisation increases even during this state shrinking process.[10] In connection with the above argument, it can be said that in the new era of globalisation, though the national phenomenon does not remain central to world political discourse, but it continues to occupy a subordinate and submerged position.[11] That means nationalism continues in its silence.

After attempting to describe the broader canvas, I come now to the fundamental idea on which I have designed my entire work. Although many secessions are taking place, yet the issue continues to remain very new as in terms of its conceptualisations different views exist which again are dependent upon the prism through which one sees the issue of secession. Secession is a very context specific issue as it changes from situation to situation.

Despite the increased frequency of secession, which can be witnessed after 1989 onwards, the subject of "secession" continues to remain a contested issue for examination. History has a number of examples of secession. Diagnoses of secession by different scholars and academician have remained more or less the same but prescriptions vary. Before coming to the case on which I have planned to work, it is important to discuss the subject matter of secession which inspite of its negativity has at its core a right to freedom but in an extreme form of demanding it at any cost.

Secession is based on either ethnic or territorial terms. It is the ethnic ground which ultimately leads to the demand for having an independent territory. The main reason for the breaking and making of a state is the suffering and pain of the people, especially the minorities of the state. Therefore, Allen Buchanan[12] and many other scholars say that secession is only justified on the ground when a particular section faced injustice, exploitation and exclusion in terms of their protection and preservation, development and participation in the decision-making process of the country or in having access to the opportunities of daily life etc. One can justify secession on these grounds. But, is secession an end to certain forms of injustice, exploitation and exclusion? The answer to this question cannot be a simple yes or no. This is because secession again brings back "injustice, exploitation and exclusion" in different forms, as a location or situation change takes place in terms of the majority and minority of people after the secession. That means, those who were the minorities in the pre-secession phase become the majorities after the secession and a new group of people takes the position of minorities there. And the truth so far is that a new group of minorities starts suffering from stereo-typical representations and faces problems again, but forms a "new ruler" who till the other day might have been their colleagues in facing the problems. So, the most important point is that even after secession, the minorities are not in a position to have access to the facilities of the state and thus secession is not an end to a problem (like the remedial argument of secession) rather it can complicate the situation more by bringing only immediate relief for some. Thus, it is important to understand why secession takes place? Often the situation before and after secession is not very different, as people lack voice and participation in both the situations. Here comes the focal point of my entire work. The lack of democratic participatory governance is the reason for which people ultimately demand secession from their polity despite knowing the fact that secession can mean loss of people and property.

Democracy in terms of free and fair and competitive elections cannot necessarily ensure good governance. Many a times even under a very strict structure of democracy, bad governance is practiced. Therefore, the important point is that "just as human development requires much more than raising incomes, similarly good governance for human development requires much more than having effective public institutions".[13] Therefore, good governance also requires fostering fair, accountable institutions that protect human rights and basic freedom. From the above discussion it is clear that there is a close link present between democracy and human development. But the particular link can be broken by a small group of people who dominate the economic and political decisions of a particular country. Because of this domination, even electoral democracies have the problem of practicing good governance. Bangladesh is an example of this type of democracy.[14] This work therefore aims to find out whether secession, which was expected to lead a democratic polity (as it happened in Bangladesh) can actually have the potential to resolve the problems of the minority insofar as their rights and human development are concerned. It also examines to what extent secession is an outcome of the lack of participatory governance. It is true that international organisation does not offer a clear-cut possibility for secession but there is always a possible chance of secession. Therefore, it is the responsibility of the government to ensure development for all and to make the government system accountable and accessible to all people so that people at large can participate in the decision-making process of government because these decisions after all affect their lives and liberty, peace and prosperity.

The main reason for choosing this particular subject of secession in the context of Bangladesh is that, in 1971, East Pakistan seceded from West Pakistan (which was not a democratic country) on the grounds that Bengali Muslims of East Pakistan (the majority) suffered exclusion (discrimination in terms of political, social, cultural, economic life) as well as domination from the Urdu speaking Muslims.[15] But after the creation of Bangladesh in 1971, which has claimed to be a democratic country since its inception in its Constitution does not prove to have been favorable to the present minorities (Hindus, Christians, etc.). Even Bangladesh has witnessed and is witnessing immense exploitation of its existing minorities.[16] Here the important point is, that merely having a democratic structure or polity in the Constitution is not enough unless it comes into practice. The status of minorities has been found to remain the same both before and after the secession.

Therefore, it is the type of government which matters most as the governance it is practising should have the potential to so flourish as to avoid not only secession but also be able to contribute towards creating a type of atmosphere where fuller realisation of citizen rights and human development is possible.[17]

Scope of Work

For this work, I have restricted my area of the study

firstly to the case study of Bangladesh, which emerged in 1971 after East Pakistan secedes from West Pakistan despite the fact that they used to share the common theological bond of Islam. Secondly, this work would look into how the government of a democratic polity and a non-democratic polity approach their minorities? And thirdly can secession really bring an opportunity for the minorities to get rid of their problems. Bangladesh religiously is a homogeneous country; because 90 per cent of people are Muslim by religion. Thus, the remaining 10 per cent of the population, who are not Muslims, become the minority. Despite the fact that the Constitution of Bangladesh adopted a democratic polity and contains many provisions for securing and protecting the minority rights, yet the minorities face immense discriminations from the so-called majorities. One may question why, despite having a democratic polity, the minorities are not safe? And more importantly, why secession, which is based on ethnic identities, does not provide a secure solution for the minorities? Secession begins with the issue of the crisis of minorities but can also end with the same problem as seen in Bangladesh.

This work also covers the theory and practice of the concept of participatory governance and inclusive institutions. The reason for focussing on participatory governance is that it can be helpful in overcoming the perceived deficiencies. Here this deficiency is related to the issue of secession. The reason, for which I have related participatory governance and secession, is that participatory governance through its fundamentally inclusive attitude or institutions is to a considerable some extent helpful in accommodating the interests of minorities as well as weakening possible secessionist tendencies.

References

1. 'Self-determination Procedure', http://www.beyondintractability.org/essay/self_determination (last accessed on 18/11/2009).
2. See Aleksandar Pavkovic and Peter Radan. *Creating New State: Theory and Practice of Secession*. Ashgate Publishing Limited, England, 2007.
3. *Ibid.,* p. 74.
4. *Ibid.,* p. 75.
5. As Amartya Sen says, that I can be, at the same time, an Asian, an Indian citizen, a Bengali with Bangladeshi ancestry, an American or British resident, an economist, a dabbler in philosophy, an author, a Sanskritist, a strong believer in secularism and democracy, a man, a feminist, a heterosexual, a defender of gay and lesbian rights, with a non-religious lifestyle, from a Hindu background, a non-Brahmin and a non-believer in an after-life (and also a non-believer in a before-life as well). Amartya Sen, *Identity and Violence: The Illusion of Destiny,* Penguin Group, New York, 2006.
6. 'Nationalism', Stanford Encyclopaedia of Philosophy, available in http://plato.standford.edu/entries/nationalism (last accessed on 15/4/2009).
7. Unlike decolonisation, secession involves dissolution or disappearance of the sovereign state from which a territory was being withdrawn. As a result of which from 1990 until 2007 secessions have led to the creation of 25 new states, which were given international recognition and admitted to the UN. This kind of argument is present in Marcelo G. Kohen (ed.), *Secession: International Law Perspectives,* Cambridge University Press, UK., 2006.
8. See Aleksandar Pavkovic and Peter Radan. *On the Way to Statehood: Secession and Globalisation,* Ashgate Publishing Limited, England, 2007.
9. Aleksandar Pavkovic and Peter Radan say that according to Lloyd Cox, in the post-Cold War era because of extended

global reach in terms of connectivity, secessionist movements have received substantial military and diplomatic support from outside of their states. This opportunity of receiving international assistance encourages secessionist moments, *Ibid.,* pp. 36–39.

10. See, *The Statesman,* April 19, 2006.
11. Eric J. Hobsbawm, *Nations and Nationalism since 1780: Programme, Myth, Reality,* Cambridge University Press, UK, 1990 and also see Lloyd Cox, "Neo-liberal Globalisation, Nationalism and changed Conditions of Possibility for Secessionist-Mobilisation' in Aleksandar Pavkovic and Peter Radan, *on the Way to Statehood: Secession and Globalisation, op. cit.*, pp. 33–49 .
12. Allen Buchanan, 'Towards A Theory of Secession', *Ethics,* Vol. 101, No. 2, 1991.
13. *Human Development Report 2002*, United Nations Development Programme (UNDP), New Delhi, 2002.
14. Promoting Democratic Governance, available in http://www.usaid.gov/jani/Chapter 1-Foreign Aid in the National Intersts.pdf (last accessed on 8/11/2009).
15. Sumit Ganguly, *Conflict Unending: India-Pakistan Tensions Since 1947*, Oxford University Press, New Delhi, 2001.
16. 'Attack on Hindu Minorities, Voice of the Asia-Pacific Human Rights Network 2001', available in http://www.hrdc.net/sahrdc/hrfeaures/HRF48.htm (last accessed on 7/11/2009).
17. *Human Development Report 2002.*

1

Issues Concerning: Political Right to Self-determination, Secession and Participatory Governance

Every concept has two parts: the theory part and the practice part. Both these parts differ in the extent to which they embody a thrust on a particular context, that is procedural or substantive or in their combination. They differ because their conceptual understanding is very different as "theory" is a set of propositions designed to explain and interpret something.[1] Which have some sort of reference in the form of present data, origin of the concept, etc. That means theory provides a framework for a concept but "practice" is the art of doing something', it means putting the plan into action. Another difference between theory and practice is that "theory" deals with a system of rules, procedures, etc., which are required to produce a desirable end. But "practice" is the end in itself as here the outcomes matter the most.

Moreover, whether it is a case of establishing desired procedures (means) or realising desired outcomes (ends) there is always a gap between the accepted theories and principles proposed and what the actual reality and practice is. This gap is because life and reality is much more complex than the prescribed abstract theories. Therefore, merely having a good principle oriented theory is not enough unless it is capable of being properly realised in society.

Keeping this distinction (i.e., between the theory/means and outcomes/practice) in mind, in this chapter and even in my entire work. It is endeavour to explore whether there is any distinction present between the theory and practice of the concept of the right to self-determination and secession and the concept of participatory governance. In order to better explain, these are extremely complex themes. I have taking up the case study of Bangladesh, which is regarded as a successful case of secession.

Coming specifically to chapter one, it is important to delineate with the theories of secession and participatory governance.

The Concept of Political Right to Self-determination and Secession

The Liberal Approach

The word "secession" which is derived from the Latin term "secessio" means an act of withdrawing from an organisation, union or especially from a political entity. Aleksandar Pavkovic and Peter Radan, define secession as a demand by the people from the host state; this demand is for getting independence from the parent state.[2] The factual situations out of which a separation or dismemberment takes place are many and varied, as they range from a break-up of a previously created entity into its previous constituents to the dissolution of a federation, to the complete fragmentation of a state into a variety of successors not being co-terminus with previous territorial units.[3]

Thus, under secession, the older state broke up and a new state is formed. The groups, which form the new state renounce the jurisdiction of the older state, of which it was a part. Where there is a separation or secession, the new state not only renounces the territorial jurisdiction of the older state but it (new state) is also free from the international treaties, rights and obligations which are applicable to the former or the parent state.[4] James Crawford defines secession as "the creation of a state by the use or threat of force".[5] Thus, Julia Dahlitz says that "the issues of secession arise when a significant portion of the population of a given territory, being a part of the state, express their wish to become a sovereign state in itself or to join another sovereign state".[6] On the basis of these two definitions, Aleksandar Pavkovic and Peter Radan identified three properties of secession:

(i) It involves the use of force; (ii) it takes place without the consent of the former state, and; (iii) creation of the new state creates its own sovereignty.[7] Because of these three properties, states are mostly opposed to secession. The reason is—the symbol of any sovereign state (a sovereign state is that state which is internally supreme and externally independent) is its control over its people and its territory. Therefore, when any state is on the verge of breaking up and creation of a new state is on the cards, that state is considered as a "failed state". The "failed state" tag is humiliation for any state. Thus, a sovereign state invariably tries to secure its existing boundaries. And for avoiding the stigma of "failed state", the former or the host state uses force to stop secession, which in a way leads to violation and degradation of human rights.

In this backdrop, secession is always considered as a negative or dirty word and more importantly it is a prohibited act in terms of the international law. It is also considered as a breach of territorial integrity and harmful to everyone engaged and concerned with it.[8] International law is based on the concept of the state. And state depends upon the foundation of sovereignty and sovereignty is nothing but a hold over the legal territory of the state. Therefore, the nature of territory becomes an important part of the study of international law.[9] According to Malcolm

N. Shaw, the concept of territory is associated with (1) "accretion"—the geographical process by which new land is formed and becomes attached to the existing land; (2) "cession"—it involves the peaceful transfer of territory from one sovereign to another and everything within the framework of a peace treaty following a war and; (3) "secession"—it is that process, in which the ethnic group claims to have a separate homeland, i.e., the establishment of a sovereign state.[10] In the case of secession, the territory does not physically walk away but the secessionist state ceases to obey the orders, laws, rules of the parent state. Therefore, secession is seen as a most disturbing political phenomenon.

The Genesis of the Concept of Secession

The number of members of the United Nations (UN) General Assembly was 51 in 1945 (establishment of UN), increased upto 149 in 1984 because of decolonisation (after the Second World War), but this number further increased to 191 and this was due to the secession process which took place after the break-up of Yugoslavia and the disintegration of the USSR in the beginning of the 1990s.

According to Andrei Kreptual, the concept of secession is not so new. He highlighted that "there are numerous historical examples of secessions (some are successful and some are failed)".[11] For example, the secession of Dutch states from the Spanish Empire in the 16th century —this secession process led to the creation of the first written document on Rightfulness of Secession—the act on secession, adopted in July 1581. This Act made secession a universal and unconditional right for all peoples." Steven Yates traced the history of secessionist argument in the Lockean tradition, i.e., when Locke in his book *"Second Treatise of Government"* said that, the citizen has the fundamental right to abolish a government, which oversteps its legislative bounds and abuses its authority. Therefore, according to Yates, Locke justified the right to revolution which is related to the 'dissolution of government'.[13] Yates again says that Locke elaborated his argument on dissolution of government by saying that the trust of the government lies in the protection of rights of the people, i.e., right to property of the citizen. When the government betrays their trust then citizens also have the power to dissolve the government.[14]

According to J.R. Graham, Locke's argument in the book the *"Second Treatise of Government"* is based on the result of the Glorious Revolution of 1689—which was a clear example of a revolutionary but lawful and peaceful transformation of government by the people, by reframing the Constitution and resetting the government.[15] Martinenko, further argues that the next important case for the right of secession is the American Revolutionary War which interpreted the right to secession as a common right for all peoples in the world.[16]

Allen Buchanan's argument on the genesis of the secession process is very different, as he is of the opinion that though liberal political philosophy has a space for the right to revolution, civil disobedience, etc., nevertheless liberal philosophy is shy about the concept of secession.[17] Therefore, according to Buchanan, secession is beyond the framework of liberal theory and he puts forward a question that if liberal political theory justifies revolution on the ground that when the state does not act on the path of justice, then why is secession not justified? Buchanan also made it clear that secession is different from revolution and emigration, because in the case of revolution people overthrow the existing government to have a different socio-political-economic order within the state. But on the other hand, in a secession process citizens free themselves from the jurisdiction of a state. Similarly, in the case of emigrants they remove themselves from the jurisdiction of a state but do not challenge state authority. However, in the case of secession, there is a rejection of state authority.[18]

Therefore, the outcome of this discussion is that, though in history there were certain instances where a group of people either revolted against the government or separated from the state.[19] Yet, a conceptual argument of justification of the secession process is basically missing. It was after the First World War when the American President Woodrow Wilson talked about the "right to self-determination", which was a part of the League of Nations in 1920, that brought to the forefront the idea of freedom of the people of a given territory to determine their own political status. This right in due course of time took the shape of a "secessionist" argument.

Self-determination, United Nations and Secession

Self-determination and secession pose a major challenge for international law—the former for its ambiguity and difficulties of operationalisation and the latter for the uncertainty of its status. Therefore, there is a constant tension between the argument endorsing the right of the people to govern themselves and the creation of a separate sovereign state.

Before the establishment of the UN in 1945, the right to self-determination was neither a political nor a legal right. It is the UN Charter of 1945, which under Articles 1(2) and 55 first recognised the "principle of equal right and self-determination of people". This particular principle became a legal right in 1960, when the UN General Assembly recognised the Declaration on the Granting of Independence to Colonial Countries and Peoples. This declaration raised two types of problems:[20]

One is that this principle gives a right to the peoples, thus it is the people who get the right of self-governance. And secondly many people relate the decolonisation process with secession. But the fact is that both are different from each other because in decolonisation, states are not a part of the imperialist state but are territorially separated by a sea or an ocean.[21] In relation to the process of decolonisation, an important principle emerges, i.e., the principle of "Utipossidetis"[22] Utipossidetis—a Latin term means "as you possess". According to this principle of international law, the territory and other property remains with its possessor at the end of a conflict. Therefore, it is a principle which is logically connected to the phenomenon of obtaining independence.[23] Thus, the controversial point of this principle is that newly-independent states should have the same borders that they had before their independence. This argument does not help in resolving the territorial conflict, rather it increases the complications. But the fact is that despite these territorial complications, the decolonisation process was quite successful.

Boutros Boutros Ghali said that the argument of self-determination is acceptable in the case of decolonisation but not in the case of secession, because if every ethnic, religious or linguistic group claim statehood, then there would be no limit to fragmentation and thus peace, security and economic well-being for all would become even more difficult to achieve.[24] Thus, the point is that the UN Charter does not endorse any type of withdrawal of territory from an existing sovereign and independent state. In connection with this argument, Anne F. Bayefsky says that, under Chapter XI and XII of the UN Charter there is a specific provision for territories of the colonial type. It is a fact though that none of the Articles under these two Chapters have the phrase "right to self-determination", but there is a provision for self-government for the people. This argument in respect of the colonial territories is not acceptable in the case of non-colonial territories. Since 1945, the international community is reluctant to accept the unilateral secession of parts of independent states.[25] The argument for secession is only acceptable when the international community and the present state recognise the new entity as a state. For example, the UN recognised Bangladesh only after Pakistan recognised Bangladesh in 1974. Thus, the scope of the UN's argument on "right to self-determination" is confined to its internal application i.e., within the existing framework of the state.[26]

From the above discussion, it is clear that, there is a legitimate claim for "political stability" against unlimited secessionist rights, but this claim does not imply that there is no right to secede.[27] There are enough arguments for accepting the claim of political stability in evaluating the scope for the exercise of the right to self-determination and yet there is also a defence for the right to reconfigure the territorial boundaries of an existing state (i.e., the right to secession). Thus, Christopher Heath Wellman argues for an "unapologetic defence of secession right", i.e., a group has a moral right to secede, so long as its political divorce will leave it and the remainder state in a position to perform the requisite political function.[28] Wellman quoted Harry Beran, David Copp, David Gauthierand Daniel Philpott. according to them "citizens ought to be allowed to redraw political boundaries in anyway that is politically feasible".[29] Allen Buchanan on the other hand offers a moral ground of justification for secession,[30] i.e., secession is only acceptable when a particular group suffers injustice where violation of political, economic and social rights are concerned, or on the ground of self-determination and nationalism.[31]

Buchanan also says that even as secession is acceptable it can be opposed on the ground that secession is incompatible with the continued existence of the remainder state and moreover it will lead to chaos if a large unit is allowed to secede then why not small ones, and if they, then why not individuals?[32]

Buchanan after suggesting the justification and opposition for the process of secession said that the issue of secession brings up two important concepts. (1) Which is the group, which has the secession right? (2) And if we are able to identify the group then does the group automatically have the right to secede? According to him in order to find a suitable answer to these two questions, we need to think first of what type of right is the right to secession?

Right to Secession is What Right?

No International law establishes secession as a legal right except a few states like St. Kitts, Nevis or Ethiopia which proclaim a right to secession).[33] However, it is also true that after 1990 when there was a rush of secessionist movements, then on many occasions international bodies and administrative or federal units recognised secession. Therefore, the question that emerges that if secession is legally acceptable, then what is its source of legality? The answer to this question is that unless the domestic law of the host state and the international law gives full legal recognition to secession, till then the secessionist state is an illegal entity.[34] Therefore, the main thrust of the secession process is not just the making of a new independent state but also to gain recognition by other states and international organisations.[35]

On the basis of this legality argument, Buchanan viewed the "secession right" as a "remedial right" not as a "primary right" based on ascriptive group theory. This means a group whose membership is defined by ascriptive characteristics, which are non-political, for example, characteristics, like common culture, language, history, etc. Associative group theory, on the other hand believes in voluntary political choice of the members of a group for deciding their politically independent status. According to the remedial right version of the right to secession, which for Buchanan also has a legal claim that is:

(1) A group has the right to secede if the physical survival of its members is threatened by actions of a state or it suffers the violation of other basic human rights.

(2) A group also has the right to secede, where its previous sovereign territory was unjustly taken over by the state.[36]

Thus, according to Buchanan, the right to secession is the last option for a group to go for. When they do not have any other option open to them, then the right to secession becomes a "remedial right"—which provides a remedy or solution to their problems. Therefore, the right to secession can be called a "qualified right", i.e., it is about a human right which can in certain circumstances be overturned by the government or by the public body where exercising of this right infringes on the rights of another person or group of people. Thus, like any qualified right, the right to secession is limitedly permissible, i.e., maximisation of this right is only possible when there is minimisation of its limitations.

Upto now, I have discussed the liberal or semi-liberal argument about the political right to self-determination and secession. But both the political right to self-determination and the issue of secession has a very different connotation when these two concepts are being discussed under the second broad approach i.e., the Marxist Approach. Therefore, in the coming few pages I would explore the Marxist understanding of the political right to self-determination and secession.

The Marxist Approach

The Marxist debate is a double-sided argument because Marxist are internationalist[37] (who practice cooperation and understanding between nations). Because of the presence of an internationalist argument, some people believe that Marxism denounces all forms of nationalism as it is problematic for international workers unity.[38] But on the other hand, it was Marx who once said a 'nation that oppresses another cannot be free' and Lenin further elaborated it by saying that a nation which is oppressed by imperialism has the right to self-determination.[39] According to Marxists, one of the consequences of imperialism was "nationalism", because the workers and peasants of the oppressed countries started revolting against this (imperialism) and thus it took the form of nationalism.[40] Therefore, Tom Lewis says that it is an important for the socialist to think about the concept of nationalism in order to approach a case for workers and peasants national liberation. This nationalism brought a new concept of state which was not based on personal allegiance but based rather on shared languages, a common territory and the perception of a group history and destiny.[41]

One of the greatest contributions of the Marxist theory on the political right to self-determination is that, they make a distinction between the nationalism of the oppressor and the nationalism of the oppressed. Because of this type of argument present within the Marxist debate, for Paul D' Amato, the possibility of equality between nations is possible.[42] According to Tom Lewis, "the nationalism of the workers belonging to an oppressor nation binds them to their rulers and does harm to themselves, while nationalism of an oppressed nation can lead them to fight back against those rulers".[43] Therefore, Tom Lewis further says that worker's unity cannot be built without workers in an imperialist or oppressor country supporting the right to self-determination of the oppressed nation.[44] So, the important point is that in order to understand the crux of nationalism, we have to study both types of nationalism faced and practiced by the people of the oppressor country and by the people of the oppressed country.

The principle of self-determination provides the people of a defined territorial unit with the right to determine their political status freely. Such determination may result in independence, integration with a neighbouring state, free association with an independent state or any other political status freely decided upon by the people concerned.[45] In order to understand this concept within the Marxist forum, it is required to look into the 1903, programme of the Congress of the Russian Social Democratic Labour Party (RSDLP) where Article 9 played an important role.[46] The 1903 Congress discussed two major points of that time. The first concerned about the "*Jewish Labour Bund*" and the second concerned the issue of Polish self-determination. The second concern was related to the national question issue, which also became the party platform, i.e., Article 9. On the basis of this Article, Lenin was in favour of the Polish people's right to self-determination from Russia.[47] This Article 9 of the 1903 Congress developed the perception of "Self-determination as a political right not a cultural right". Lenin defended this Article 9 because he believed that the right to self-determination for oppressed nations remains "absolutely" essential for the Social Democrats, for the sake of the basic principle of democracy.[48] For Lenin the right to self-determination implies the coming of a democratic system and also includes the stopping of an undemocratic practice to support the case of secession.[49] That means Socialists must be hostile towards the use of force in any form by the dominant nation in respect of the nation that wishes to secede politically because for them. They will only address the demand for secession of a given territory where it is settled on the basis of universal, direct and equal vote of the population of that territory by secret ballot.[50] Sy Landy says that the major outcome of Lenin's argument was that the entire fight for the right to self-determination was meant for democratic demands to free, educate and politically unify the proletariat—outside the oppressed nation as well as within.[51] That means the fight of the proletariat for the right to self-determination was nothing but a part of their struggle for having consistent democracy.[52]

Tom Lewis in his article "Marxism and Nationalism" says that Lenin's idea that the notion of self-determination expresses a political right, as opposed to an economic and cultural right was a heated issue because it brought out opposition from two different directions. One from Otto Bauer (the Austro-Marxists), who advocated cultural interpretation of the right to self-determination and second from Rosa Luxemburg, the Polish Marxist, according to whom economic development almost made it impossible to have the exercise of the right to self-determination.[53]

According to Otto Bauer (who advocated the cultural interpretation of the right to self-determination) the nation is the totality of human beings bound together through a common destiny into a community of character. [54] According to Munck, for Bauer, the nation is a product of history.[55] According to Bauer, "individuals belonging to our nation actually experience the world differently from individuals of another nation, because of the unique cultural environment that has determined their thought and behaviour".[56] This shows that for Bauer, culture plays an important role in defining the relationship between an individual and the nation. For Bauer, social, historical and cultural factors plays an important role in describing human existence because these are the factors which determine the uniqueness of various nationalities and nationalism. Because of this viewpoint, according to Munck, Bauer attacked the economic deterministic angle of Marxism and became an advocate of the importance of the cultural dimension.

Bauer advocated "Cultural National Autonomy". According to this, it will give self-determination to people for development of their cultures.[57] For Bauer, this cultural national autonomy would become an alternative for eradicating inequalities against the minorities. But on the other hand for Lenin this would intensify isolation and impoverishment of national minorities.[58] The second type of opposition for Leninist discourse came from the "radical left" like Rosa Luxemburg and Trotsky. They were the supporters of proletarian internationalism in opposition to the idea of national separation advocated by Lenin.[59] According to Luxemburg, imperialism and internationalisation of capitalism made national struggle impossible because the world economy became so powerful that national independence has in fact no meaning.[60] Rosa Luxemburg in the article "The National Question and Autonomy" says that the right to self-determination is an abstract and metaphysical right. According to her this right to self-determination leads to the support for the right to secession and for her this further leads to support for bourgeois nationalism because all these rights tend to the creation of a bourgeois state.[61] Specifically on the Polish issue, for Rosa Luxemburg independence was a utopian idea. A shift in her perspective came when she wrote the *JUNIUS PAMPHET* in 1915—where to some extent she adopted the right to self-determination, on the ground that—socialism gives to every people the right of independence and the freedom of independent control of their own destiny.[62] After saying this she also made it clear that this self-determination could not be exercised within existing capitalist states, particularly colonialist states.[63] Lenin was against Luxemburg's argument on nationalism and the right to self-determination because for Lenin this type of argument completely divides oppressed nations and oppressor ones. Another point of opposition was that Luxemburg looked at every thing from the world economic point of view and ignored the political dynamics.[64] Horace B. Davis in the book *"Towards a Marxist Theory of Nationalism"* says that although it is true that Luxemburg never wanted a general principle of self-determination yet it is also true that she wanted a guarantee of self-government and cultural autonomy to her people (i.e., for the people of Poland). Lenin who supported the self-government concept says that though Luxemburg advocated the demand for having autonomy but it was restricted to Poland alone. And Davis says that for Lenin every case (people who demand the right to self-determination) has its own uniqueness. Therefore, one has to look from that point of view and one cannot have a generalistic and fixed conception.[65]

Trotsky (another radical Marxist) had a very economistic and cultural point of view towards the concept of the nation. According to Horace B. Davis and Michael Lowy, for Trotsky the nation in the future would exist as a cultural, ideological and psychological phenomenon.[66] Therefore, according to Michael Lowy, Trotsky[67] like Rosa Luxemburg overlooked the political dimension of the concept of nation and only focussed on "proletarian internationalism"—where the economic dimension plays an important role. Lowy further says that Trotsky had one commonality with Lenin as he (Trotsky) supported the right to self-determination as one of the conditions for having peace between nations. But the problematic part was that Trotsky neither elaborated the proper definition of the term internationalism nor did he elaborate much on the right to self-determination. Lenin's successor as leader, Stalin did attempt a major but flawed theorisation of nationalism and eventually emerged as an aggressive Russian nationalist.[68]

The world Communist movement shifted from internationalism to nationalism under the impact of the degeneration of the revolution of 1917 in Russia and the rise of Stalin, who developed the idea of "national Bolshevism.[69] Stalin's definition of the nation is that if there is a common language, territory, economic life and psychic formation then one can have a nation.[70] He in fact made no distinction between the oppressor nationalism and the nationalism of the oppressed nation.[71] On one hand, he opened the door for the idea of having distinct national struggles for socialism and on the other hand he rejected the notion of national-cultural autonomy but did not explain how nations could be formed at all when the nationalities were all mixed up together. [72]

From the above discussion it seems that Lenin's theory of nationalism and the right to self-determination is the most systematic way of approaching these concepts under the broad spectrum of the Marxist debate.[73] Lenin's defence of the right to self-determination opened the door for incorporating nationalism within the Marxist platform of internationalism, by relating democracy and socialism with the concept of nationalism. [74]

The "Leninist Formula", i.e., the "right of self-determination upto and including secession refers to the category of any oppressed nationality."[75] Achin Vanaik in his book *'India in a Changing World'* explained the Leninist formula by pointing out that, the "Leninist formula was seen as justified because it represented an extension of democracy" especially since it referred to the "oppressed nationality".[76] Lenin was basically concerned because after the Bolshevik Revolution and the formation of the Soviet Union the neighbouring Central region was also experiencing bourgeois revolutions and national movements which were spreading to the Russia dominated co-nationals.[77]

However, after the Russian Revolution Lenin reformulated the "right to self-determination as a right to equal states of every nationality within the larger political unit, the Soviet Federation".[78] According to Mark Cowling, there were two main reasons behind Lenin's reformulation of his earlier argument. Firstly, which of the many groups to be found within the former Tsarist Empire were nations and should be supported in attaining self-determination if they so wished? And secondly, how should the Bolshevik party be organised given the divisions between nationalities?

In the book *'India in a Changing World'*, Achin Vanaik says that, Lenin's theory politically useful though it was and certainly democratic in its spirit cannot avoid problems regarding its application. What makes a nationality? How does one make a judgement whether a nationality is oppressed or not? For both liberal (and semi-liberal) and the Marxist approach the right to self-determination and the right to secession is more or less related with the "remedial right" theory. According to the Achin Vanaik the right to self-determination is a particular kind of "collective right"[79]. While some collective rights must assume or be reducible to an individual right, for example the collective right of free expression must mean an individual right to free expression, this cannot be the case for the collective right to self-determination where individuals and sub-groups can choose not to be part of that collective entity.[80] Both liberal and Marxist approaches have not adequately addressed the complications caused by this distinction within the overall category of collective rights as it pertains to the issue of the right to self-determination. Though, it is true that both the approaches look at the right to self-determination and the right to secession from the remedial point of view, that is, as a remedy from a non-democratic situation to move towards a democratic situation, nevertheless the Marxist, particularly Leninist attitude to the issue of the right to self-determination—respect for the right to self-determination for an oppressed nationality, upto and including the right to secession but with safeguards for national minorities, is both more democratic in spirit and more flexible politically than many a liberal inspired approach.

After analysing both the approaches (Liberal and Marxist), it is clear that despite their differences one common point that emerges, from both the approaches is that the tendency towards secession is inherent in "the political right to self-determination" even if practical fulfillment of that right often falls short of secession.

The Concept of Participatory Governance

In order to understand the concept of participatory governance, we need to look into the two terms that constitute it. The word "participatory" is related to the word "participation" which means "to take a part or share". And the word "governance" means "the act or manner of governing".[81] So, when these two words came together and formed the term "participatory governance", then it means participation or taking part in the act or functioning of the government. The participants are common people, various actors in civil society and other stakeholders.

The issue of "participation" is important because "growth" only is not the sole indicator of progress. Rather, "development" should be the major indicator of progress. And development must be woven around the people and refer to the empowerment of individuals and groups. And this empowerment of the people is possible only by bringing people's participation directly into the functioning of the government. Governance is the practicing part of government. So, it follows that governance must be decentralised and participatory in nature. This would give a sense of belonging to the people who are the participants and then there is maximum chance for having a well-developed society where everyone is able to have optimisation of their capacities and the best means to achieve their well-being.

And only under a such well-organised situation, one can find that a positive correlation exists between two important indicators of "progress", i.e., economic growth and development. Once development is understood in this sense, as Sen's capability approach demands (based on an alternative to the standard economic frameworks for thinking about poverty, inequality and human development), then substantive democracy becomes an imperative. Because according to Rajeev Bhargav and Ashok Acharya, *"Political Theory an Introduction"*, democratic arrangements play a constructive role by allowing the conceptualisation of what actually constitutes economic needs. Thus, only a democratic governance system has the capability to advance the cause of human development for all the common people.

In the notion of a "democratic governance system", it seems that the term democracy plays an important role because democracy is that form of government where the realisation of people's participation is possible. When we say democracy is that form of government where the realisation of people's participation is possible, then we are looking into the substantive dimension of democracy, which believes in redistributive justice, enhancing human capabilities and entitlements (education, health, infrastructure etc.), social capital or associated factors (trust, values, norms), human rights and respect for peoples' dignities and truly democratic governance (participation, accountability, efficacy, transparency, etc.).[82]

We have two types of justifications for making democracy our sole concern that is, to say democracy has both an "intrinsic" and an "instrumental" value.[83] When we are saying that democracy has an intrinsic value, then we are indicating that it (democracy) is essential for its own sake; that means it is the fairest way of giving expression to equality among citizens.[84] On the other hand, when we are saying that democracy has an instrumental value also, then we are indicating that it (democracy) serves as a means to help others. For example in a democracy more than one political leader can participate and this helps the people, who have more options while electing the political leaders, and this further helps by making the people more politically responsible.[85]

It is quite clear that the purpose of human development is to increase people's range of choices because a country's development should be "people-centred."[86] Democracy is primarily linked with the political freedoms which people of a democratic country enjoy. There are five indicators of political freedom. They are:[87]

1. Personal Security (Absence of arrest and detention, torture or cruel treatment or punishment, arbitrary killings, disappearances).

2. Rule of Law (fair and public hearings, competent, independent and impartial tribune, legal counsel, review of conviction).
3. Considerable freedom of expression.
4. Political participation (free and fair elections, continuity of the democratic system, community and local decision-making bodies).
5. Equality of opportunity (legal guarantees against violence or harassment of particular groups, political and economic participation for all).

From the five indicators of political freedom one thing is clear that the "continuity of democratic system" is the main and the core point because only under a democratic system can people enjoy these freedoms, as democracy works through the two key principles of "popular control" (that means popular control over public decision-making to make it effective and inclusive) and "political equality" (by removing obstacles in terms of gender, ethnicity, religion, caste, language etc.),—that means equal exercise of citizenship right.[88] Thus, these two principles are the guiding factors of democracy assessment. The more the presence of these two, the more the chance of having a democratic system.

It is clear from the above discussion that the presence of a democratic governance system is an essential requirement for overall human development. But the idea of having democracy is not so simple because over the years, it (democracy) takes many forms, like direct procedural and substantive, representative, deliberative, participatory and others. All these forms of democracy have their own special characteristics. Like the direct democracy or which is regarded as the oldest form of democracy, it is basically concerned about direct participation of the people into the functioning of the government. Direct democracy believes in the supremacy of the people. On the other hand, procedural democracy basically emphasises the procedures and institutions of democracy and substantive democracy works on the idea that it is necessary to have a society of truly equal citizens, who are politically engaged, tolerant of different opinions and ways of life and also have an equal voice in choosing their rulers and holding them accountable.[89] The concept of representative democracy comes in opposition to direct form of democracy because it believes that a direct form of democracy is not possible in large societies. Therefore, it is a better option to have an elected representative who works on behalf of the people. But some people are of the opinion that even this representative democracy does not prove to be an adequate democratic form, therefore some other form of democracy is required. In this backdrop, deliberative democracy came into being.

According to Simone Chambers[90] democratic theory took a completely new turn with the coming of the deliberative concept of democracy, because the deliberative concept of democracy has its roots in reasoned dialogue and deliberation.[91] The freedom to speak, to engage in political conversation, to discuss political issues and to deliberate about the common good is the hallmark of a democracy.[92] With the coming of deliberative democracy the voting centric-democracy changes to talk-centric democracy because deliberative democracy believe in the importance of the communicative process.[93]

Joshua Cohen, one of the greatest advocates of deliberative democracy says one of the important justifications for the ideal of deliberative democracy is the presence of the procedures of political deliberations, that means deliberative democracy accommodates the "principle of participation.[94] Supporters of deliberative democracy say that because of the presence of public deliberation and dialogue, deliberative democracy offers an inclusive and fair society. Despite the deliberative democracy having so many good points yet today a new form of democracy is getting significance, that is, participatory democracy.

Participatory Democracy believes in active citizens participation. Participation is important not only in decision-making but also it is a way of protecting private interests and ensuring good government.[95] Participatory democracy offers a more egalitarian approach towards the concept of democracy as it believes in both vertical and horizontal political talk and participation.[96] And because of the presence of both vertical and horizontal forms of participation, participatory democracy believes in both quantity and quality. Thus, participatory democracy may be regarded as "the modern version of government by discussion."[97] Tom Atlee says, according to Elizabeth Meehan, participatory approach "brings together people who have the direct knowledge of the problem" thus able to provide a good solution for avoiding it. And with people's participation the institutions became more accountable, transparent, and fair.

The most important thing coming after the discussion on participatory democracy is that it is based on the principles of liberty and equality.[98] And on these two principles the desire for self-determination is based, i.e., "how self-rule is to be achieved through the models of democracy".[99] According to Helena Catt participatory democracy provides an alternative through which self-government can be achieved by the people as they make the decisions, for example by allowing the people to vote on an important issue in a referendum.[100] Here lies the uniqueness of the participatory form of democracy—as it involves all the forms of democracy in one or the other way. Participatory democracy is directly linked to the deliberative form as both believe in public talk, and participation is a kind of deliberation. But the importance of participatory model lies in the word "participation", which has an intrinsic value, which broadens the spectrum of peoples actually participating. The participatory model is even linked with direct democracy, as it uses many of the methods of direct democracy to have better public participation. Participatory democracy has connection with representative democracy since it cannot do without the application of the representative principle even though it goes beyond it. By having linkages with various forms of democracy the participatory model seems to be the most favourable one. Because it mediates between citizen participation, authorisation, representation, accountability, transparency, responsiveness and solidarity.[101] It is true that, theoretically the participatory model has all the good points. But to what extent it can enter the realm of the practical is a matter of concern.

This practical realm is the governance part. This governance part is important because good governance is the first criteria for achieving human development. And governance for human development is much more than merely having effective[102] institutions and rules. Therefore, a synthesis between participating governance is required, i.e., participatory democratic governance.

With this understanding, we are moving back to the theoretical understanding of the political right to self-determination and secession once again where it is clear that whether it is the liberal approach or the Marxist approach secession can often be justified in the name of democracy promotion. This hardly resolves all problems or issues that emerge, theoretical or practical but it does provide some kind of baseline for guiding and judging policy formation and public action by various social actors including the state. In most cases, people go for secession because there is the absence of a democratic system or of democratic alternatives in addressing their problems. The more participatory is the character of a democracy, the less likely is it that a group of people will seek to decide their political status independently from their current state.

References

1. *The New Collins Concise English Dictionary,* William Collins Sons & Co. Ltd, England, 1982.
2. See Aleksandar Pavkovic and Peter Radan, *Creating New States Secession,* Ashgate Publishing Limited, England, 2007, pp. 1–4.
3. See Malcolm N. Shaw, *International Law,* Cambridge University Press, U.K., 2005.
4. *Ibid.,* pp. 878 –879.
5. Aleksandar Pavkovic and Peter Radan, *op. cit.,* p. 6.
6. *Ibid.,* p. 6.
7. *Ibid.,* pp. 1–6.
8. *Ibid.,* pp. 5–16 and M.N. Shaw, *op. cit.,* pp. 399–420.
9. M.N. Shaw, *op. cit.*, pp. 419–421.
10. *Ibid.,* pp. 419–442.
11. See Andrei Kreptul, 'The Constitutional Right to Secession in Political Theory and History', *Journal of Libertarian Studies,* Vol. 17, No. 4, Fall 2003, pp. 39–100.
12. See Steven Yates, 'When is Political Divorce Justified?' in David Gordon (ed.), *Secession, State and Liberty,* Transaction Publishers, New Jersey, 2009, pp. 39–40.
13. *Ibid.,* pp. 39–40.
14. *Ibid.,* pp. 38–40.
15. See Andrei Kreptual, *op. cit.,* pp. 40–57.
16. *Ibid.,* p. 63.
17. Buchanan says that liberal philosophy values liberty and autonomy, diversity and value only legitimate political authority. See Allen Buchanan, *Secession: The Morality of Political Divorce Form Fort Sumter to Lithuania and Quebec,* Westview Press, Boulder, 1991; 'Theories of Secession', *Philosophy and Public Affairs,* Vol. 6, No. I, 1997, pp. 33–61; 'Towards a Theory of Secession', *Ethics,* Vol.101, No. 2, 1991, pp. 322–342.

18. Allen Buchanan, 'Towards a Theory of Secession', pp. 326–327.
19. See V. P. Nanda, 'Self-determination Under International Law: Validity of Claims of Secede' 13 Case Western Reserve, *Journal of International Law*, 1981.
20. See Aleksandar Pavkovic and Peter Radan, *op. cit.,* p. 20.
21. See M.N. Shaw, *op. cit.,* p. 2–5 and *Ibid.,* pp. 20–23.
22. See Suzanne Lalonde, *Determining Boundaries* in *Conflicted World: The Role of UTI-POSSIDEITIES,* McGill-Queen's University Press, Canada, 2002.
23. *Ibid.,* pp. 2–10.
24. Quoted from Aleksandar Pavkovic and Peter Radan, 'In Pursuit of Sovereignty and Self- Determination: Peoples, States and Secession in the International Order', *Macquire Law Journal,* Vol. 3, 2003.
25. Anne F. Bayefsky, *Self-determination in International Law: Quebec and Lessons Learned,* Kulwer Law International, Netherland, 2000.
26. *Ibid.,* p. 496.
27. See Allen Buchanan,'A Theory of Secession', *op. cit.,* pp. 31– 61.
28. Christopher Heath Wellman, *A Theory of Secession: The Case for Political Self-determination,* Cambridge University Press, New York, 2005, pp. 2–11.
29. *Ibid.,* p. 34.
30. See Allen Buchanan, 'Towards a Theory of Secession', *op. cit.,* pp. 322–342.
31. *Ibid.,* pp. 323–327.
32. *Ibid.,* pp. 323–339.
33. Aleksandar Pavkovic and Peter Radan, *Creating New States: Theory and Practice of Secession. op. cit.,* pp. 5–21.
34. *Ibid.,* p. 29.
35. *Ibid.,* p. 33.

36. Allen Buchanan, 'Towards a Theory of Secession', *op. cit.,* pp. 31–61.
37. Marx and Engels says that "Workers of the World Unite".
38. Paul D'Amato, 'The Meaning of Marxism: Marxist and the Right to Self-determination", June 21, 2002, available in http://socialistworker.org/2002-2/411/411_09Self Determination. shtml(last accessed on 12/17/09).
39. See Horace B. Davis, *Towards A Marxist Theory of Nationalism,* monthly Review Press, New York, 1978; Tom Lewis, 'Marxism and Nationalism', *International Socialist Review,* Issue 13, Aug-Sep. 2000, available in http://www.isreview.org/issues/13/marxism_nationalism_part1.shtml (last accessed on *12/17/09)* and also see Paul D' Amato, 'The Meaning of Marxism: Marxist and the Right to Self-determination', June 21, 2002, available in http://socialistworker.org/2002-*2/411/411*—09–SelfDetermination.shtml(last accessed on *12/17/09).*
40. Tom Lewis, 'Marxism and Nationalism', *International Socialist Review,* Issue 13, Aug-Sep.2000, available in http://www.isreview.org/issues/13/marxism_nationalism_part1.shtml (last accessed on *12/17/09).*
41. *Ibid.,* p. 1.
42. Equality between nations can be established by granting the oppressed nation the right to self-determination because this is the only way through which workers of the oppressed countries unite with the workers of the oppressor country.
43. Chris Harman, 'The Return of the National Question', *International Socialism* 56, Autumn 1992, p. 18.
44. Paul'D Amato, *op. cit.,* pp. 1–2.
45. See 'The Subject of International Law' in Malcolm N. Shaw, *op. cit.,* pp. 175–241.
46. Right of Self-determination for all nations included within the bounds of the state (Article 9, Programme of the Russian Social Democratic Labour Party 1903).

47. The Polish Socialist Democrats wanted national independence from Russia for the emancipation of the Polish workers. Though, it was true that at that time economically Poland and Russia was united but this integration disturb their (Poland) national identity.
48. Tom Lewis, *op. cit.,* p. 4.
49. *Ibid.,* p. 5.
50. *Ibid.,* p. 5.
51. Sy Landy, 'Self-determination and Military Defence: The Marxist Method', *Proletarian Revolution 59, Summer* 1999 (Transcribed, edited and formated by Damon Maxwell and David Walters to 2008 for the Encyclopaedia of Trotskyism, available to http://www.marxist.org/history/etol/writers/landy/1999/xx/military.htm, last accessed on 12/11/09).
52. *Ibid.,* p. 1.
53. Tom Lewis, *op. cit.,* p. 6.
54. Ronnie Munck, 'Otto Bauer: Towards A Marxist Theory of Nationalism', *Capital* and *Class,* 1985, Vol. 9, No. 1, 1985, pp. 84–97.
55. Firstly because all individuals resides within history and secondly peoples of a nation are bound together in a nation by different means and different ways which also emerge at various stages of historical development.
56. Tom Lewis, *op. cit.,* p. 6.
57. Ronnie Munck, *op. cit.,* pp. 87–89.
58. See *Ibid.,* pp. 85–95 and also see Tom Lewis *op. cit.,* pp. 2–5.
59. See The Marxist Debate on self-determination in Michael Lowy, Fatherland or Motherland. Essay on National question, Pluto Press, London, 1998, p. 30.
60. See *Ibid.,* pp. 30–33 and also see David McNally, 'Marxism, Nationalism and National Struggles Today' (*A Discussion Document for New Socialist Group,* 1996, available in http://www.newsocialist.org/index.php? option=com_content&

view=article&id=1488 Itemid=75, last accessed on *12/22/09).*

61. Michael Lowy, *op. cit.,* pp. 31–32.
62. *Ibid.,* p. 33.
63. *Ibid.,* p. 33.
64. David McNally, 'Marxism, Nationalism and National Struggles Today' (A *Discussion Document for New Socialist Group,* 1996, available in http://www.newsocialist.orgindex.php? option=com–content&yiew=article&id=1488Itemid= 75,last accessed on *12/22/09).*
65. Horace B. Davis. *op. cit.,* p. 83.
66. See *Ibid.,* pp. 83–85 and Michael Lowy, *op. cit.,* p. 36.
67. Michael Lowy, *op. cit.,* pp. 36–37.
68. Horace B. Davis, *op. cit.,* pp. 85–86.
69. David McNally, 'Marxism, Nationalism and National Struggles Today' (*A Discussion Document for New Socialist Group,* 1996, available in http://www.newsocialist.org/index.php?option=com content&view_article&id_1488 Itemid_75, last accessed on *12/22/09).*
70. Michael Lowy, *op. cit.,* p. 38 and Horace B. David, *op. cit.,* p. 71.
71. Michael Lowy, *op. cit.,* p. 39 and Horace B. David, *op. cit.,* p. 70.
72. See Horace B. David, *op. cit.,* p. 72 and also see David McNally, 'Marxism, Nationalism and National Struggles Today' (*A Discussion Document for New Socialist Group,* 1996, available in http://www.newsocialist.org/index.php?_option=comcontent&view=article&id=14881temid=75 last accessed on 12/22/09).
73. See Sy Landy, *op. cit.,* pp. 1–3.
74. Horace B. Davis, *op. cit.,* p. 86.
75. See Lenin on 'What is Meant by self-determination of Nations?',(available in http://www.marxist.org/archive/Lenin/works/1914/self-det/ch0l.htm. last accessed on

12/12/09). And also look into Achin Vanaik, *India in a Changing World, Orient Longman,* India, 1995.

76. See 'Problems Old and New: The Uncertain Future', in Achin Vanaik, *op. cit.,* pp. 85–102.
77. See Mark Cowling, 'Marx and Engels, Marxism and The Nation' in Karl Marx and Mark Cowling, *Tile Communist Manifesto: New Interpretations,* Edinburgh University Press, Edinburgh, 1998.
78. Quoted from *Comparative Politics: Issues and Trends* by Indira Gandhi National Open University, School of Social Science, New Delhi, 2006.
79. Achin Vanaik, *op. cit.,* p. 106.
80. *Ibid.,* pp. 106–108.
81. See *The New Collins Concise English Dictionary,* William Collins Sons & Co. Ltd, England, 1982.
82. See *India: Democracy and Development Book* - 2 by Indira Gandhi National Open University, School of Social Sciences, New Delhi, 2004, p. 107.
83. See The New Collins Concise English Dictionary.
84. See *Political Theory*—I, by Indira Gandhi National Open University, School of Social Sciences, New Delhi, 2005, pp. 31–32.
85. *Ibid.,* p. 31.
86. See 'Manual For Training of Trainers on Human Development Part-l', prepared by Dr. Arabinda Ghose, Planning Commission—United Nations Development Programme (UNDP) sponsored project "Strengthening State Plans for Human Development", Administrative Training Institute, Government of West Bengal.
87. *Ibid.,* pp. 7–8.
88. See Handbook on Democracy Assessment, Kluwer Low International, 2002.
89. See *Political Theory*-1, p. 33.
90. See Simone Chambers, 'Deliberative Democratic Theory', *Annual Review of Political Science,* 2003 p. 307.

91. See Scott London, 'Tele-democracy vs. Deliberative Democracy: A Comparative Look at Two Models of Public Talk', *Journal of Interpersonal Computing and Technology,* Vol. 3, No. 2, April 1995, pp. 33–55.
92. The energy of democratic idea lies in the way the citizens have the capacity to speak and think.
93. Simone Chamber, *op. cit.,*p. 308.
94. The deliberative democracy justification lies in exercise of public power—have equal rights of participation, including rights of voting, association and political expression etc. Elaborated by Joshna Cohen, 'Procedure and Substance in Deliberative Democracy' in Thomas Christiano (ed.) *Philosophy and Democracy: An Anthropology.*
95. See *Political Theory*-1, p. 33.
96. Vertical and horizontal participation means talk between the political offices and citizen and between the citizens respectively.
97. Tom Atlee on Elizabeth Meehan's 'Reconstituting Politics: Democracy Unbound', available in http://co-intellieenceorl:/CIPOL ParticDelibDemoc.htm (last accessed on 01/01/10).
98. Helena Catt, *Democracy in Practice,* Routledge, Oxon, 1999.
99. *Ibid.,* p. 12.
100. *Ibid.,* pp. 12–13.
101. Handbook Oil Democracy Assessment, Kluwer Low International, 2002.
102. *Human Development Report 2002,* United Nations Development Programme (UNDP), Oxford University Press, New Delhi, 2002.

2

The Breaking of Pakistan vis-a-vis the Making of Bangladesh: Bangladesh's Liberation War of 1971

In the post-colonial period, the birth of Bangladesh in 1971 was one of the first instance of an ethnic-linguistic nationalist movements[1]. Which was resulted into the breaking of Pakistan on linguistic basis, i.e., West Pakistan for Urdu speaking Muslims (script is based on Arabic alphabet) and East Pakistan (now Bangladesh) for the Bengali speaking Muslims (script is based on Devnagari). This breaking of Pakistan and making of Bangladesh is marked by the India-Pakistan war of 1971, which is also known or called as 'Liberation War of Bangladesh'. According to scholars like Sumit Ganguly, Raunaq Jahan, Badrudding Umar, *et al.*,[2] the genesis of Bangladesh liberation war was rooted in the partition of India in 1947 as shown in Fig. 2.1, which resulted into the coming of two sovereign states primarily on the basis of religion. The British rule divided India into India (based on Hindu majority) and Pakistan (based on Muslim majority). When India and Pakistan separated in 1947, then East Bengal chose to join the dominion of Pakistan and thus became one of the province of Pakistan but it was separated from another province of Pakistan by about more than 1000 km

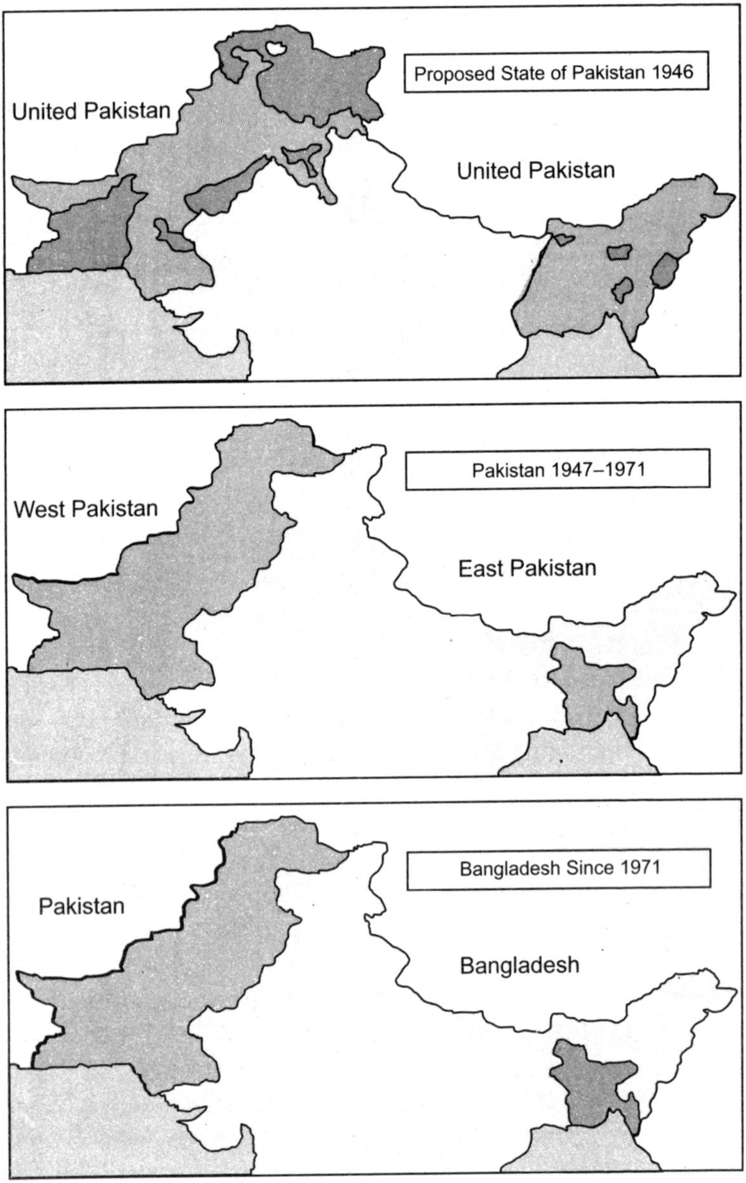

Fig. 2.1. The Birth of Bangladesh in 1971.

of Indian territory.[3] Therefore, physically, psychologically and emotionally, East Pakistan was separated from West Pakistan before the emergence of partition and it remained so even after the emergence of Pakistan in 1947. They (East Pakistan and West Pakistan) had only one thing in common, that is their common religion. Beyond religion, neither West Pakistan nor East Pakistan had any common ground for having emotional attachment towards each other. They had so many differences and distinctions in terms of geographical location, social and cultural beliefs and practices, economic and political influence. As a result, religious commonality could not provide a sustainable bond between the two and ultimately East Pakistan seceded from West Pakistan. This particular secession has a long history. In this chapter, primary aim is to highlight the details of those events, which ultimately led to the secession of East Pakistan from West Pakistan.

History of Bengal after the Coming of British Rule to 1947 (Partition of India)

Bengal was a huge province and Dacca (now Dhaka) was the seat of Nawabs when it was absorbed by the Mughal Empire in the sixteenth century.[4] Portuguese traders and missionaries were the first Europeans, who reached Bengal in the later half of the fifteenth century and they were followed by representatives of the Dutch, the French and the British East India Companies.[5] All these European countries came in India primarily for economic interests especially for enhancing their trade by making India as a base both for procuring their raw materials and selling finished good products. It was the British who not only enhanced their trade in India but also slowly and gradually grew and built a political hold on the Indian territories. After the decline of the Mughal empire, Bengal witnessed the coming of independent provincial Nawabs. But after the Battle of Plassey in 1757[6] (led to defeat of Nawab Siraj-udulah), the British crown finally took control over the territory of Bengal and started expanding their control on the Indian sub-continent by making Calcutta their centre. Thus, by the late eighteenth and early nineteenth century, the British rule almost covered the entire Indian territory.

Bengal which was a major province received a major-set back under the British colonial regime.[7] The impact of British colonial rule was so devastating that it not only disintegrated the social fabric of Bengal but also destroyed its prosperous trade and business status. The late nineteenth century witnessed the rise of nationalism throughout British-controlled India which led to the coming up of two major religious groups in India—Hindus and Muslims who jointly participated in the revolt of 1857[8] or The First War of Indian Independence. As a result of this revolt in 1859, the British Crown replaced the East Indian Company (which actually extended British dominion from Bengal further towards the West)[9]. In 1885, the Indian National Congress was founded by Indian and British rule in such a way that it emerged as a Hindu dominated party which ignored the values of the Muslim community. In this way, British rule carried out its famous policy of "divide and rule". This policy of divide and rule is based on the idea of communalism[10], which culminated not only in the partition of Bengal in 1905, but also resulted in the formation of the All India Muslim League in 1906.

Lord Curzon (the main person who brought about the partition of Bengal in 1905) said that the partition of Bengal was required because Bengal was geographically too large a province to be properly managed. But the real motive behind this partition was a division of two religious communities Hindus (belonging to West Bengal) and Muslims (belonging to East Bengal).[11] The 19th century, therefore saw the rise of communalism and communal hatred among Hindus and Muslims. This particular division brought about significant changes in the relationship between the Hindu and the Muslim elite groups, i.e., *Bhadralok* and *Ashraf* class respectively.[12]

Before the division, the Hindu *Bhadralok* and the Muslim Ashraf class were involved in conflict because the Hindu *Bhadralok* had a very neglected indifferent attitude towards Islamic Culture.[13] And after the partition, this tension increased tremendously because the Muslim community welcomed the partition of Bengal as it helped in expanding their educational, economic and political opportunities (which according to the Muslim Community was ignored by the Hindu Community).[14] But on the other hand, the Hindu *Bhadralok* community opposed the partition in the name of Bengal identity.[15] This mobilisation of the Muslim Community resulted in the formation of All India Muslim League in 1906[16] under the guidance of Nawab Salimullah and his fellow supporters. The formation of the Muslim League was a clear-cut example of the rise of an all Indian Muslim political organisation vis-a-vis Congress (which for the Muslim community was a Hindu organisation). With the coming of the Congress and the Muslim League as two distinct political organisations, the feelings of separateness among the two religious communities intensified further. This communal tension got further accelerated with the coming of the Government of India Act 1909.[17] In the Government of India Act 1909 or the Morley Minto Reform, for the first time, the idea of "separate electorates" was introduced for the Muslim community. So, a sense of nationalism which was required at that time to commonly fight against British colonial rule could not grow. Rather the said Act not only disturbed the social fabric but also contributed in making these two communities 'hostile towards each other'. This 'anti-feeling' became so extreme that though in 1911 British rule again reunited Bengal yet a common bond did not emerge and with the passage of time, the gap between these two communities increased further. Although both the Congress and the Muslim League supported the idea of India's freedom and independence, they never came together in their approach towards addressing various issues. As result of which the idea of a separate Muslim state gained popularity among the Indian Muslims. So, the conclusion is that British rule succeeded in their target of enforcing the policy of divide and rule.

Throughout the period of British rule, Britishers maintained a different set of attitudes towards the Hindu and Muslim community respectively. Therefore, whatever efforts had been put up by the nationalist groups (freedom fighters) to reunite the Hindu and Muslim community could not bridge the gap that got created between the two communities. Apart from Britishers divide and rule policy, the nature of Indian nationalism was also responsible for deepening the gap between Hindu and Muslim communities. Because this type of nationalism, which developed in India at that time was tilted towards Hindu Nationalism (developed uncler the umbrella of Indian National Congress) rather than secular nationalism.[18] According to Mushirul Hasan this Hindu nationalism forced the Muslim community to think in the direction of having a different "Muslim Nationhood".[19] This idea of "Muslim Nationhood" gave a completely different meaning to the concept of 'nation', 'nationalism' and 'community' which further led to the mixture of political nationalism with religious nationalism.[20]

In this background of religious nationalism when the Muslim League suffered a decisive defeat in the 1936 election, the only dream they (Muslim people) had was the creation of a Muslim State-based on the identity of Muslim culture. Since then the Bengali Muslim voted for Muslim nationalism rather than for Indian or Bengali nationalism[21]. Therefore, the important point here is to note that the demand for having a separate Muslim state was primarily supported by the Bengali Muslims (people who ultimately became the natives of East Pakistan after the partition of

India into India and Pakistan in 1947). In this background the Lahore Declaration of 1940 by Jinnah provided an immediate turn to India's freedom struggle, as he gave his idea of a "Two Nation Theory"[22], and therefore demanded an independent Muslim state where Muslims would be in majority. This particular idea floated by the Muslim League got majority support not only from Indian Muslims but also from a group of Hindu nationalists, as Hindu nationalists wanted to preserve the Hindu heritage.[23]

Savarkar's doctrine of Hindutva was based on the concept of Hindu racial supremacy and thus he wanted to establish a *Hindu Rastra*. Therefore, when Jinnah gave his Two Nation Theory then Savarkar said that "I have no quarrel with Mr Jinnah's Two Nation Theory.... It is a historical fact that Hindus and Muslims are two nations."[24] This particular saying of Savarkar gave open support to religious communalism over secular nationalism. All this led to the growth of the Muslim League's influence at provincial level which was clearly visible in the provincial election of 1946[25] when it (Muslim League) got the majority of the Muslim seats contested in Bengal. This particular victory gave many Muslims a sense of national identity and a belief in their right to self-determination. This further helped them to make an equal claim vis-a-vis the Hindu community, i.e., parity of representation with the Hindus at the centre became a principle demand for the Muslim community.[26] After the election it was clear that India would get her independence by paying the price of partition. Therefore, many plans and proposal (Cabinet Mission Plan,[27] Wavells Breakdown Plan[28], Mountbatten's Plan Balkan,[29] etc.) were introduced between 1946 to 1947 to decide on the process of partition. But none of these plans were accepted because of the clash between Congress and Muslim League. After the failure of all these plans Mountbatten suggested an alternative plan on 3rd June 1947[30] which proposed the transfer of power to two dominion governments India and Pakistan and the date for transfer of power was declared as 14th and 15th August 1947.

This decision not only brought freedom and partition for India but also had a great significance because the province of Bengal faced its second partition within the same century. Which completely changed the face of Bengal and sowed the seed for the secession of East Pakistan eventually resulting in the emergence of an independent sovereign country—Bangladesh in 1971.

From the Formation of East Pakistan to the Birth of Bangladesh 1947 to 1971

As discussed above, the partition of India in 1947 witnessed the partition of Bengal again. This proved very costly not only for Bengal province but also for India-Pakistan relations (i.e., Hindu-Muslim relations). When India was partitioned Bengal was divided among the two new dominions. The Western part of the province became West Bengal a state in India and the Eastern part became East Bengal part of Pakistan. This division was based on the Hindu-Muslim division, so it is clear that it was the common religion, which tied up the two distinct units of Pakistan despite the fact that they were separated territorially. East Bengal was the only one among the five provinces which formed united Pakistan, which was in the Eastern zone and the other four provinces (West Punjab, Sindh, Baluchistan and North-West Frontier Province) were positioned on the Western side thus becoming West Pakistan. Therefore, since the beginning this territorial-geographical division created a psychological blockage between the two wings of the then Pakistan, because of which there arose a difference in interest articulation among the peoples of East Pakistan and West Pakistan. Thus, slowly and gradually the religious nationalism changed in the direction of a growing Bengali cultural nationalism in the Eastern wing of Pakistan. Nationalism, which means a sense of belongingness and togetherness, develops among the people when they share a common history, geography, ethnicity, religion, language and culture.[31] But unfortunately, there were no such common linkages present between East Pakistan and West Pakistan apart from Islam. Thus, it can be said that the "Islam" which had became a catchword for uniting the two wings of Pakistan could not retain its charm for a longer period of time. Rather, it was increasingly replaced by the rise of secular non-religious arguments which included the spirit of tolerance, justice, mutual accommodation by political leadership, etc.[32] This new development led to a weakening of the possibility of having a common nationalism in Pakistan. And simultaneously the growing discontent in the two wings on political, social, economic and cultural grounds culminated in the development of deeper disparities and differences between them.

Although it is true that Bengal gave maximum support to Jinnah for his struggle for the creation of the separate state of Pakistan. Yet within a short period of time because of multiple unfavourable factors, the demand for creation of a separate state became a popular slogan. There is a belief that in a democracy it is the majority, which have no fear of being discriminated or excluded. But this was not the case in the former state of Pakistan (1947 to 1971). Though, the people of East Bengal were in a majority, they witnessed all sorts of problems like absence of regional autonomy, disproportionately fever places in the civil services, lack of guarantees of economic freedoms or protection of their culture etc.[33] According to G.W. Choudhury[34] this indifferent attitude towards the majority led to the rise of Bengali sub-nationalism that finally resulted in the creation of Bangladesh.

Factors Responsible for the Rise of Growing Disparities between East Pakistan and West Pakistan

(a) Political Sphere and the Difference in Attitude: Since the very beginning of the creation of Pakistan, her two wings or units never shared an equal level of political participation in the centre of the governmental structure. It was West Pakistan which used to dominate the Eastern front. And this domination of one wing over the other became a major factor for the separation of East Pakistan from West Pakistan.

Although it was true that after the partition of India in 1947, Pakistan adopted the British model of parliamentary system but it was equally true that the model was ill-equipped for her and she never accommodated to it.[35] Pakistan even failed to adopt a federal Constitution.[36] This failure of adopting a parliamentary system and a federal Constitution led to a weakening of "democracy" as a result of which there was neither a single general election nor provincial election during the 1947 to 1958 period.[37] In spite of various drawbacks, mentioned above, the situation was still manageable and under control as long as Jinnah was alive. But after the assassination of Jinnah (the first Prime Minister of Pakistan) political power got concentrated into the hands of the President of Pakistan which later brought about bureaucratic rule and a military regime.[38] One of the main reasons for the rise of power elites was the absence of a Constitution.[39] And even after the formation of a Constitution, there was always a clash between the presidential versus parliamentary democracy.[40] It was in West Pakistan where political power actually remained. As a result of which the Bengal is had a very minimal role/ voice in major matters (political, economic, defence, diplomatic) and all important posts in the administration were held by the West Pakistanis. The Bengali's were poorly represented in the army and other sectors.[41]

As the Bengali's were under-represented in the military of Pakistan, therefore from the defence point of view they (peoples of East Pakistan) faced unequal treatment. For example, in the India-Pakistan war of 1965, East Pakistan was totally cut off for 17 days from any military support from West Pakistan.[42] This particular incident made it clear that East Pakistanis were defenceless, despite the Pakistan government spending a huge amount of money on defence. This sense of military insecurity forced the peoples of East Pakistan to develop their own defence force. This demand was supported by the National Awami Party and radical students. They gave the slogan "*Joy Bangla*."[43]

The people of East Pakistan received strong support for their own issues from Sheikh Mujibur Rahman, the leader of the Awami League, when he said," the question of autonomy appears to be more important after the war (India-Pakistan war of 1965). Time has come for making East Pakistan self-sufficient in all respects". Mujibur's leadership finally became influential when he launched his Six-point Programme for full regional autonomy in East Pakistan in 1966. The demands put forward under the Six-Point Programme were:[44]

(1) The Constitution should create a federation of Pakistan in a true sense on the basis of the Lahore Resolution and for a parliamentary form of Government-based on the supremacy of a directly elected legislature on the basis of universal adult franchise.

(2) The federal Government should deal with only two subjects: defence and foreign affairs. All residuary powers should be vested in the federating states.

(3) There should be either two separate convertible currencies for two wings or one currency with two separate reserve banks.

(4) The power of taxation and revenue collection shall be vested in the federating units. The federal government will receive a share to meet its financial objection.

(5) Economic disparities between the two wings shall disappear through a series of economic, fiscal and legal reforms.

(6) A militia or paramilitary force must be created in East Pakistan, which at present has no defence of its own.

When this Six-point Programme was launched, Pakistan witnessed multiple complexities at that time under Ayub Khan's leadership. Ayub was against the Six-point Programme while Zulfikar Ali Bhutto was engaged in forming another political party programme in West Pakistan called Pakistan's People's Party.(PPP) and this party was against Ayub's regime and Tashkent Declaration (signed after 1965 War).[45] This was the time when Pakistan witnessed two different types of demands in terms of political format.[46] One was the idea of a centralised government and the second was a demand for provincial autonomy." Around this time another major event took place which brought hatred into the minds of the East Pakistanis because Mujibur Rahman was intentionally incriminated in the Agartala conspiracy case;[47] and was sent into a West Pakistan jail. But because of lack of evidences he was released. This particular incident was a kind of insult for the people of East Pakistan and it culminated in the development of strong hatred and bitterness against the central political leadership of Pakistan. After Mujibur's release, it was decided that this Six-point Programme would be discussed in detail after the election. This unpleasant political atmosphere reached its climax when for the first time the national election held in 1970. Mujiburs Awami League got the majority of seats. The party won 167 seats out of 169 seats allotted to East Pakistan and thus established a majority in the National Assembly.[48] This victory gave the party the legal or constitutional right to form a government. But opposition leader Zulfikar Ali Bhutto refused to accept this and to allow Mujibur to became the Prime Minister of Paksitan. He even denied Mujiburs Six-point Programme. In this background, on 7th March 1971, Mujibur declared Nation-

Wide-Strike. And in his speech he said "our struggle is for our freedom. Our struggle is for our independence."[49]

(b) Economic Disparities between East Pakistan and West Pakistan

The economic basis of Bengali nationalism in East Pakistan was centered on the issue of "economic exploitation" faced by the peoples of East Pakistan vis-a-vis the peoples of West Pakistan. Authors like Sirajul Islam,[50] G. W. Choudhury[51] et al. say that the most serious challenge and the root cause of the weakening of Pakistan's nationalism was growing economic-financial disparities between the two wings of Pakistan. It was true that after the formation of Pakistan in 1947, significant efforts had been made towards economic development. But unfortunately United Pakistan did not practice a policy of balanced economic growth. As a result, West Pakistan developed more than East Pakistan because West Pakistan was the centre of political dominance. Examples of economic imbalances were—a good percentage of the budget was spent on defence (concentrated in West Pakistan); a larger share of development expenditure as well as of foreign aid and loans went to West Pakistan. Though, East Pakistan exports of jute were a major foreign exchange earner, spending favoured West Pakistan.[52] As a result of these differences, West Pakistan witnessed faster economic growth as compared to East Pakistan.[53]

Table 2.1: Economic Growth Rate between East Pakistan and West Pakistan

Year	*Average Growth Rate*	
	Percentage of East Pakistan	*Percentage of West Pakistan*
1949-50	1.9	2.7
1969-70	4.3	6.4

Source: Sirajul Islam, *History of Bangladesh: 1704–1971, Economic History,* Asiatic Society of Bangladesh, Dhaka, 1992.

This faster economic growth increased disparities between the two wings of East and West Pakistan.

Table 2.2 Disparity Reason between East Pakistan and West Pakistan

Sl. No.	*Year*	*East Pakistan*	*West Pakistan*	*Disparity (2-1)*	*Disparity Ratio 2-1/2×100*
1.	1949-50	288	351	63	21.9
2.	1954-55	294	365	71	24.1
3.	1959-60	277	367	90	32.5
4.	1964-65	303	440	137	45.2
5.	1969-70	331	553	202	61.0

Source: Quoted from Report of the Panel of Economisation, the Fourth Five Year Plan of Pakistan (Report of West Pakistan Economist) in Sirajul Islam, *History of Bangladesh: 1704–1971, Economic History,* Asiatic Society of Bangladesh, Dhaka, 1992.

The above table shows that the economic disparity was so deep within the system of Pakistan that the disparity ratio of 21.9 per cent reached 61 per cent by 1970. Therefore, the Bengali economists of East Pakistan supported the Awami League's Six-point Programme, which aimed to secure economic rights for East Pakistan's people. Thus, we can conclude that economic exploitation was one of the major reasons for promoting a sense of deprivation that finally became a driving force behind the rise of a Bengali nationalism demanding self-rule in the form of the creation of Bangladesh.'[54]

(c) Issue of Bengali Language Identity and Protection of Bengali Culture

For the people of East Pakistan, apart from their religion they had a strong affinity towards their language. They joined Pakistan for protection of their identity. But after partition they realised that even the Central government (West Pakistan) of Pakistan was not in a mood to protect their ethnic identity. The best example of this indifferent attitude was the forceful imposition of Arabic script in Bengali language. Therefore, the members of East Pakistan made significant demands for protection of their language "Bengali", i.e., they demanded that Bengali should be recognised as one of the state languages.[55] But the leaders of West Pakistan denied this particular demand on the grounds that "Pakistan has been created because of the demand of hundred million Muslims in the subcontinent and the language of a hundred million Muslims is Urdu".[56]

Actually, the genesis of the Bengali language issue was located into Jinnah's speech of 1948 where he said "let me make it clear to you that the state language of Pakistan is going to be Urdu and no other language". This particular statement became a serious bone of contention for the Bengalis who wanted to have Bengali as one of the state language. The demand for Bengali language got its momentum on 21st February (*Ekushe* February) 1952, when young students demonstrating for getting recognition of their mother tongue Bangla were shot at by the police.[57] This particular incident sowed the seeds of the idea of Bangladesh. Though, in 1954, the Constituent Assembly decided to have both Bengali and Urdu as languages of Pakistan and after the formation of the Constitution in 1956, the East Pakistan people got Constitutional security for protection of their language, nonetheless the Bengali people were never satisfied because the government of Pakistan hardly followed the Constitutional path of parliamentary democracy. Rather they believed in presidential-military rule which was centered in West Pakistan.

This language domination of West Pakistan government was cultural domination for the people of East Pakistan. For the Bengali Muslims prior to the partition of India they were culturally dominated by the Hindu community and after partition, by the Muslim Urdu speaking community. So, Bengali Muslims started losing their faith in the Urdu speaking Muslims and they again came closer to the Bengali Hindus of West Bengal (state of India) because of the common Bengali culture. The identity of being Bengali was so dominant among the minds of Bengali Muslims of East Pakistan that they proclaimed" "*Aamra Hindu Ba Musalman Jamon Satya, Taar Cheyo Baro Satya Aamra Bangali. Ae Kono Aadorshier Katha Naye, Ekti Bastob Satya. Ja Prakriti Nijer Haathe Aamander Cheharae O Bhashaye Bangalitayer Emon Chap Mere Diyeche Je, Mala - Tilak - Tikite Ba Tupi-Lungi- Daarite Dhakbar Joeti Nei*".[58] This phrase indicates that for Bengalis, their Bengali identity was so embedded into their nature that even the religious symbols could not supplant it for a longer period of time. Thus, we can say that for the birth of Bangladesh, the cultural - linguistic consciousness of the Bengali community played a vital role.

(d) Educational Disparity between the two Wings of Pakistan

There was a clear disparity in how the government of Pakistan implemented educational policies in her two wings. From the very beginning of the independence of Pakistan, her two units had contrasted educational endowments. For example, East Pakistan had more primary and secondary schools than West Pakistan in 1948.[59] But by 1971, the scenario was just the opposite and the West Pakistan Government followed a semi-colonial policy towards the people of East Pakistan. This was clearly evident in the distribution of economic resources targetted towards educational facilities. According to M. Niaz Asadullah,[60]" educational developments in a federal system depend upon the funds allocated by the Central government to her provincial governments". And in the case of East Pakistan this was tremendously low in relation to her population. For example, East Pakistan received only 20 per cent of the Central government development expenditure (despite having 60 per cent of country's population). This was later[61] increased somewhat to 36 per cent and remained so till 1970. West Pakistan received the maximum benefits.

(e) Civil—Military Relations

Pakistan is always busy handling the difficult relationship between the military chief and the elected civilian government. The relationship between these two groups was unequal from the very beginning of the independence of Pakistan. The two wings East Pakistan and West Pakistan never had a balanced position when military chiefs and elected civilians came to share the power because both military chiefs and top elected civilians belonged to West Pakistan. In united Pakistan, it was military rule which ruled the roast. As this military extended its reach it led to political fragmentation and non-democratic arrangements.[62]

In the first phase of independent Pakistan, the military controlled the decision-making process (defence and security affairs). Because of this the idea of parity of representation[63], one unit bill[64], etc., type of policies came. But after 1958 when Iskander Mirza declared Martial Law in 1958 and appointed Ayub Khan as Chief Martial Law Administrator, Pakistan witnessed complete overthrow of civilian government which culminated in authoritarian and centralised rule, centered in West Pakistan. This martial law rule continued till 1962 when a Constitution introduced 'civilianised military rule'. Then from 1966 to 1971 President Yahya Khan ruled Pakistan. Though, he abolished Ayub's Constitution he continued the martial law till he handed over his post to Zulfikar Ali Bhutto.[65] So, the point to be highlighted is that because of this centralised military dictatorship the peoples of East Pakistan suffered a lot which led to the rise of a secessionist movement. Military rule could not become an accepted alternative to civilian rule in the whole of Pakistan.

(f) 1970 Cyclone in East Pakistan

During November of 1970, a severe cyclone and tidal wave hit the areas of East Pakistan. It is regarded as the deadliest tropical cyclone ever because it affected millions of lives and massively destroyed property. Despite the serious consequences of the natural calamity the Central government took a long time to start the relief operation.[66] And because of East and West controversy and differences, the long-term relief planning was also inadequate.[67] This neglected attitude of the Central government made it clear to the people of East Pakistan that they had to resolve their problems on their own. The injustice visible in handling even this natural calamity also gave support to the idea of self-statehood for the people of East Pakistan.

All these factors completely shattered the dream of Jinnah to have a United Muslim state, i.e., Pakistan. Jinnah who was the founder of Pakistan had an idealistic vision of Pakistan which was based on the idea of secular, democratic, respect for ethnic or linguistic difference[68], he himself did not retain all these ideas for a longer period of time and his successors were more concerned to develop a strong regime centered in West Pakistan.

Declaration of Independence of Bangladesh and the Role of India

As discussed in the above paragraphs how exploited the people of East Pakistan were by the Central government based in West Pakistan. This exploitation crossed every limit of patience when after the national election no action was taken on Mujibur Six-point Programme nor was Mujibur given the power to form the government. Under the leadership of President Yahya Khan, both the party leaders discussed the political future of Pakistan but the talks failed and disorder prevailed which reached its climax on 25th March 1971 (remembered and regarded as the Black Day in the history of Bangladesh), when the West

Pakistan military cracked down on unarmed innocent civilians of East Pakistan.[69] This planned military action carried out by the West Pakistan Army was named Operation Searchlight. The main motive of Operation Searchlight was to curb the Bengali nationalist movement. As a reaction to this on that night itself Mujibur Rahman, the leader of the Bangladesh Awami League signed an official declaration of independence of Bangladesh.[70] Bangladesh declared independence on 26th March 1971, and the declaration was broadcasted by Major Ziaur Rahman on 27th March 1971. It resulted in the arrest of Mujibur Rahman and the practice of genocide against the people of East Pakistan by the West Pakistan Army. This genocide is regarded as one of the world's worst genocides because it took according to some estimate more than one million lives of Bengalis and perhaps up to three millions lives.[71] It was the Bengali women who paid the maximum price as a result of the genocide because they were dishonoured (were raped) by the soldiers of the West Pakistan army. The West Pakistan army carried out mass killings, looting of houses and raping of women as a practice to teach lessons to the people of East Pakistan. By attacking Bengali Muslim women, West Pakistan again expressed their contempt for the culture of East Pakistan as women are regarded as the guardians of culture, where culture is understood as an established 'way of life'.

When the proclamation of independence was issued, on behalf of Mujibur, other party members of the Awami League immediately formed the Government of Bangladesh in exile in Mujib Nagar and declared Mujibur as the President.[72] Since Mujibur was in jail at that time Syed Nazrul Islam became the acting President. Syed Nazrul and other members then joined the Liberation Army of Bangladesh Mukti Bahini[73] under the leadership of Colonel Osmani. This was the time when the Indian government got involved in the liberation war because the people of Bangladesh fled to Indian territories in order to have shelter. The West Pakistan's Army seized the homes and properties of Awami League members, and they carried out inhuman atrocities and brutalities against the peoples of East Pakistan. Thus, they had no choice but to come to India for shelter. In the first phase, the Indian government provided food and shelter to the refugees but later India provided military support to the Bangladesh Armed Force Mukti Bahini[74] (Indian government provide arms, ammunitions and soldiers). On 27th March 1971, Indira Gandhi (Prime Minister of India) expressed her full support to the Bangladesh liberation war and thus opened the India-Bangladesh border, to allow the Bangladeshi refugees in. Along with the border support, the government of West Bengal, Bihar, Assam, Meghalaya and Tripura established refugee camps.[75] These shelter camps were used to train the members of Mukti Bahini. And it was the Indian force which gave training and assistance to these people. Mukti Bahini followed the tactics of guerilla war[76] against the West Pakistan army. Bangladesh was divided into 11 sectors[77] and each sector was placed under the command of trained officers. These sectors worked under the supervision of Indian trained officers. Apart from Mukti Bahini some independent forces also participated in the liberation war (Mujib Bahini organised in India under Major General Oban of Indian Army and Students of Awami League and others).

In this liberation war of Bangladesh, Leftist groups also played an important role (despite the fact that Leftist were not unified on the national question). Though, the pro-Peking Marxists unitedly opposed the crackdown of the Yahya regime yet they were divided among themselves. One group was supporting the Awami League (supported by Indian and Soviet Army) and a second group viewed the Awami League as a bourgeois nationalist party whose main objective was to establish the dominance of the Bengali bourgeoisie.[78] Despite this difference within the Leftists, during the war the East-Pakistan Communist Party (Marxist-Leninist) was formed by Mohammad Toaha and

Abdul Haq. But because of internal controversy[79] the party split into two, whereby Abdul Haq gave support to the West Pakistani Army against Indian aggression, and on the other hand Toaha's party was loyal to the Awami League and backed them in their struggle for independence. However, because of this split these Leftist groups were on two different sides but both of them were of the opinion that the West Pakistani Army should stop their brutal attitude towards the Bengalis.[80]

By the end of October 1971, it was clear that a war would definitely take place between West Pakistan's Army and Mukti Bahini (supported by Indian troops). On 21st November 1971, Indian troops moved towards East Pakistan, thus on 23rd November 1971 President Yahya Khan declared emergency[81] in Pakistan. And finally the war took place when on 3rd December 1971, Pakistan declared war against India. Though, it is true that the India-Pakistan war did not last for a longer period of time but even within this short period it involved the then super powers (USSR and USA) and the neighbouring country (China). When India supported the liberation War of Bangladesh, simultaneously she (India) had signed a peace-treaty of 20 years with USSR which was based on the idea of friendship and mutual cooperation among India and Soviet Union. The treaty was obviously an indication that USSR would help India for her support towards Bangladesh's liberation War. With this treaty Soviet Union got involved in the war. The Soviet Union supplied tanks, missiles, ammunition to India which India transferred to the Bangladesh Army against the West Pakistan Army.[82] After the Soviet Union's involvement in the war, the USA joined the side of Pakistan[83] and supported Pakistan with economic and military aid. But when USA realised that West Pakistan had almost lost control over East Pakistan, then USA suspended their sending of military aid but they continued food aid programmes. The entire liberation war took a different shape when the USA sent her Seventh

Fleet[84] to the Bay of Bengal against the Soviet Union's missile cruiser. Because both the super powers got involved in it the Cold War tension became a major concern. During this time China also supplied military and economic aid to Pakistan. But despite the situation of extreme tension the war ended on 16th December 1971. On this day, the West Pakistan Army under the command of Lt. General Niazi surrendered unconditionally to the Indian Army and Mukti Bahini under the command of Lt. General Aurora. This surrender of the West Pakistan Army, finally politically separated East Pakistan from West Pakistan. On 22nd December 1971 the members of the Bangladesh government who were in exile reached Dhaka and on 23rd December 1971 in the first cabinet meeting of liberated/independent Bangladesh, "Bengali" was declared as an official language.[85]

The Idea of Humanitarian Assistance, the Role of UN and India in the Liberation War of Bangladesh

Any issue which is not only restricted to the affected area but spread out to other areas, then has an international relevance, like the Bangladesh liberation War. East Pakistan was the affected area yet it involved other countries. Thus, from a national issue during 1971 it became an international concern. It has already discussed how economically, politically, culturally, militarily the people of East Pakistan were dominated by the people of West Pakistan, which ultimately led to the rise of the Bangladesh liberation movement. Earlier the people of East Pakistan only wanted federal autonomy in their region but with military suppression their demand for autonomy changed to a demand for complete independence.[86]

According to the theory of "the right to self-determination", it is an inherent right of all peoples that they can freely determine their political status and they can also pursue their economic, social and cultural development.[87] This definition indicates that the theory of self-determination provides an inter-relation between people and territory, that means rights of the people on a particular territory. But this right is not for all collective groups who wanted to have their self-determination, on their territory, because if it is open to all, then everyday hundreds of these types of groups would come and make a claim for it. Therefore, the self-determination right is related to national identity. According to the UN Charter a plural society which is composed of various racial, linguistic or religious groups sharing a common national identity can make such a claim.[88] By supporting this claim the Charter is supporting the idea of secularism, multi-racialism and multi-lingualism.[89] From this angle, East Pakistan's people justified their claim because their distinctive national identity was discriminated against and subordinated by West Pakistan and thus for East Pakistan this discrimination and domination is a violation of human rights against the basic rules of the UN.

The UN was established for protection and promotion of and respect for human rights and fundamental freedom for all regardless of race, colour, creed, sex, religion or language.[90] Therefore, the UN Charter has declared that they have faith in fundamental human rights because it is about a person's dignity and which she/he should get by virtue of being human.[91] The principle of equal rights and self-determination of peoples has been recognised as basic human rights, therefore if people are denied of them then it is against the UN Charter. Simultaneously, Article 2(4) of the Charter prohibits the threat or use of force against the territorial integrity or political independence of any state or in any other manner inconsistent with the purposes of the UN Charter.[92] This indicates that sovereignty allows States to arrange their internal issues independently without any external interference.[93] And according to Article 2(7) of UN Charter, nothing contained in the present Charter which authorises the UN to intervene in matters which are essentially within the domestic jurisdiction of any state.[94] Now comes the actual complication that whether or not the UN and any other country has the right to interfere in the internal affairs of the state, despite the fact that the government may be violating human rights (as in the East Pakistan case). According to non-interventionists[95], and restrictionists[96] any intervention in the affairs of sovereign state in the name of humanitarian assistance breaches the UN Charter clause under Article 2(4) and 2(7). Therefore, there is a popular belief that when a country intervenes on the basis of violation of human rights or giving humanitarian assistance then they are clandestinely pursuing their "national interest" or fulfilling their "political objectives."[97] Thus, a doubt has been there that this intervention may disturb the principle of sovereignty. Hence, the issue of sovereignty has a nexus with the concept of humanitarian assistance on the ground of protection of human rights. India's military intervention in the affairs of East Pakistan in 1971 is an example of this nexus. India's intervention not only led to the end of West Pakistan's brutal killings of the Bengali peoples of East Pakistan, rather this particular intervention brought about independence for the people of East Pakistan, (i.e., birth of Bangladesh in 1971) which further led to the territorial emasculation of Pakistan. Moreover, the most important point here is that, India justified her intervention in East Pakistan on the grounds of humanitarian assistance.[98] So, the issue is that when humanitarian assistance involves military intervention into another State then can we call it a justified act or not? Is military intervention acceptable?

Military intervention refers to those wars which are not directed towards self-defence rather it is based on the motive of human rescue or preventing unwanted political or military developments in other states.[99] On the basis of this definition military intervention includes two diversified viewpoints. Firstly, it is matter of interference in another's sovereignty, and secondly the victim country[100] demands this intervention as an aid for their helpless situation. Those who supports military intervention arguments, also support just war theory, which is based on two basic principles:[101]

1. *Jus ad bellum* (JAB) no nation or political group should go to war unless it is morally justified.
2. *Jus in bello* (JIB) the conduct of the war should be governed by pertinent moral principles.

Whatever trying to put forward is that if a group of people faced extermination, execution and immense discrimination from their government, then military intervention by other countries becomes the alternative to get-out-of that situation. India's intervention in East Pakistan is an example of such intervention irrespective of whatever other strategic motives, e.g., seeing an opportunity to weaken its strategic "enemy" Pakistan, might have been. But the main problem in India's intervention was that it simultaneously involved the then superpowers (USA and USSR) and India herself witnessed the India-Pakistan War of 1971. Therefore, the atmosphere of that time was really out of control at one point, and moreover the Hindu-Muslim clash which was already there got greater acceleration after this war. Even for the UN (during 1971), it was a major concern that it should maintain a balance between minimisation of violence and maximisation of human rights and dignity by respecting the clauses of the UN Charter.[102] Because on one hand there were equal rights and the right to self-determination for East Pakistan and on the other hand there was the issue of territorial integrity of Pakistan[103], and both of these principles are recognised under the UN Charter. A further predicament of the UN was that the demand of the people of East Pakistan was not only restricted to equal rights and right to self-determination, rather it included the demand for territorial separation from the existing state Pakistan. Therefore, East

Pakistan's demand was "secessionist self-determination,[104] and not just self-determination.

Because of the decolonisation process there were many small and large states that emerged as independent sovereign states. Pakistan after independence adopted and practiced the same political colonised rule against her fellow citizens of East Pakistan. Therefore, the dissident group (the people of East Pakistan) in fact had no option and thus secession became the only choice for them on the basis of remedial right theory of secession (as discussed in chapter-1). Thus, despite UN support for the principle of territorial integrity, in the East Pakistan case the UN came to a conclusion that it is a product of anti-colonial self-determination[105] and moreover the most important point is that it is humans for whom all provisions and procedures are being made. Therefore, if they are the sufferers then this undivided national sovereignty claim has no meaning. Then the primary concern is to give protection to them (people). this is the reason for why UN support was finally given to the claim of the East Pakistan people. After the 1971 war the Secretary-General of the UN, U. Thant said:[106]

A ... problem which often confronts us, and to which as yet no acceptable answer has been found in the provisions of the Charter, is conflict between the principles of territorial integrity of sovereign states and the assertion of the right to self-determination, and even secession, by a large group within a sovereign state. Hence again, as in the case of human rights, a dangerous deadlock can paralyse the ability of the United Nations to help those involved.

After the war of liberation, the most important issue was recognition of Bangladesh by other countries as well as by the UN. India was the first country, which gave recognition to the Bangladesh government on 6th December 1971 (the time when war was going on). By early 1972, UK, Soviet Union and many other countries gave recognition to Bangladesh. When this process of recognition speeded up then the Prime Minister of Pakistan Bhutto offered Mujibur the power of governing a United Pakistan.[107] But in response to it Mujibur said "I do not want Pakistan." Bangladesh is now a reality:[108] And finally on 1974 the Government of Pakistan gave recognition to Bangladesh and after that the Security Council of UN approved the application of Bangladesh. Thus, Bangladesh got admission to UN with this recognition finally the Liberation War was over and now Bangladesh is one of the leading South Asian Countries.

References

1. See Rounaq Jahan, *Bangladesh Promise and Performance*, UPOL, Dhaka, 2004.
2. Sumit Ganguly, *Conflict Unending: India-Pakistan Tensions since* 1947, Oxford University Press, New Delhi, 2001; Badruddin Umar, *The Emergence of Bangladesh* Vol. 1: *Class Struggle in East Pakistan* (1947–1958), Oxford University Press, Karachi, 2004.
3. 'History of East Pakistan 1947–1971', available in http://www.Administrator/LocalSettings/Temp/Temporary (last accessed on 2/11/09).
4. "History: British Rule to East Pakistan 1757-1970", available in http://bangladeshtravell.com/2009/09/01/history-british-rule-to-east-pakistan-1757-1970 (last accessed on *04/14/10).*
5. "History: British Rule to East Pakistan 1757–1970", available in http://bangladeshtravell.com/2009/09/01/history-british-rule-to-east-pakistan-1757-1970 (last accessed on *04/14/10).*
6. The Battle of Plassey took place in 1757 between Siraj-ud-Daulah and the British East India Company. Siraj-ud-Daulah was the last independent Nawab thus after the battle the East India Company got the complete control.

7. All the achievements made during the previous centuries in the field of arts and crafts, manufactures and industries, education and administration were overturned under the impact of colonial rule. See more details in BANGLAPEDIA: *'Nationalism'* National Encyclopaedia of Bangladesh, 2006.
8. The Revolt of 1857 or the Sepoy Mutiny was considered as the first war of Indian independence because it was a great uprising against the British rule. As the Sepoys refused to touch the greased cartridges they were court martialed. This sparked the war. Though, it was a great uprising yet it failed because it was not so well organised. But the matter of concern was that the revolt witnessed the coming of all religious communities under one forum, see more in http://www.indianetzone.com_26/the_revolt/857_india_history.htm (last accessed on 04/12/10).
9. 'The Indian Mutiny of 1857–1858: Causes and Consequences', *Stabroke News,* 15th April, 2007.
10. Communalism means the tendency of the people to perceive their interest as identical with those of their religious groups, the tendency to regard the values and activities of members of others religious groups as alien or antagonistic. That means religious groups always have a tendency to be involved in conflicts. See Sirajul Islam (ed.), *History of Bangladesh 1704–1971: Political History,* Asiatic Society of Bangladesh, Dhaka, 1992.
11. Lord Curzon officially justified the idea of partition in Bengal in 1905 on administrative grounds-province was too large and the Eastern region needed proper care. The new province was known as Eastern Assam with capital in Dhaka. As this Eastern zone comprised overwhelmingly the Bengali Muslim population, the hitherto minority became a majority in their new provinces. This partition promoted the extreme feeling of sectarianism. For more details see Niki-Seth-Smith, 'Partition of Bengal 1905: History of the Partition of Bengal under British Rule 1905 to 1911', available in http://www.indianetzone.com/14/partitionbengal1905.htm (last accessed on 02/17/10) and

also see 'New World Encyclopaedia: Organising Knowledge for Happiness, Prosperity and World Peace', available in http://www.newworldencyclopedia.org_entry_Partition-of-Bengal (last accessed on 02/12/10).

12. Sirajullslam, *op. cit.,* p. 311.
13. The Hindu community named the Muslim community as slaughterer, cow-killers, meat-eaters, etc., *ibid.,* p. 310.
14. *Ibid.,* p. 311.
15. The Hindu community was against the partition because rise of opportunities for the Muslims means decrease of their own opportunities. *Ibid.,* pp. 311–312 and more in Banglapedia: *'Nationalism',* National Encyclopaedia of Bangladesh, 2006.
16. In December 1906, Nawab Salimullah Khan presented a proposal for the establishment of political party to have a community. This proposal resulted into the formation of Muslim League in 1906. The three factors which forced the Muslim community to have a distinct political organisation of their own were:
    1. Sir Syed Ahmed Khan's advice that a distinct political institution can only protect the interests of the Muslim Community.
    2. Hindu agitation against the partition of Bengal.
    3. The development of Hindu religious revivalism which according to the Muslim community was hostile and anti towards their (Muslim community) religious belief. See more details in http://www.storyofpakistan.com/articletext.asp/artid=A031 (last accessed on *02/18/10).* And Baldev Bishnoi's, 'All India Muslim League (AIML) and the Formation of Pakistan', available in http://www.rajput botherhood.com/knowledge-hub/history/all-India-muslim-aiml-and-the-fomlation-of-pakistan.html (last accessed on 02117/10).
17. The main points of Morley Minto Reforms:
    1. The law allowed the Indians to take part in the

election of the various legislative councils in India for the first time.

2. Introduction of electoral reforms based on the pattern of parliamentary system.
3. For the first time "separate electorates" for the Muslims community was introduced under this act, which means only Muslims should vote for the Muslim candidates.

This particular idea of separate electorate became a point of tension throughout the freedom struggle of India. Because the British rule deliberately encouraged the communal difference between the Hindu and Muslim community and this tension got more and more intensification with the coming of Government of India Act 1919 and Government of India Act 1935, because both these Acts furthermore divided these two communities gap, available In http://www.indianetzone.com/14/government_india_net_1909.htm (last accessed on 02/18/10) .

18. Mushirul Hasan (ed.), *India's Partition: Process, Strategy and Mobilisation,* Oxford University Press, New Delhi, 2001, pp. 1-3 and Sekhar Bandyopadhya, *From Plassey to Partition: A History of Modem India.* Orient Black Swan, India, p. 262.
19. Sekhar Bandyopadhya, *op. cit.,* pp. 262–264.
20. Mushirul Hasan, *India Partitioned: The Other Face of Freedom* Vol. 1, Lotus Collection, New Delhi, 1995, pp. 26–27.
21. Banglapedla: *'Nationalism',* National Encyclopaedia of Bangladesh, 2006.
22. The formation of Pakistan was based on the logic that the Muslims are entirely separate from the Hindus in every respect. They form an ideological community with divine guidance for every field of human life, and it is a dictate

of their faith to establish where they (Muslims) can rule according to the laws and norms prescribed in their religion. This particular theory is known as "Two Nation Theory" (see details in Maulana Maududi, 'Two Nation Theory and The Struggle for Pakistan' by Abdul Majid Jaffry, available in http://www.witness-pioneer.org/vil/Articles/politics/maududi2.html(last accessed on 02/20/10). and John McLeod, The History of India, Greenwood Publishing Group, 2002.

Because of this idea that Muslim should have a different state-based on their own religion, according to Uzma Maroof the creation of Pakistan was not an accidental process rather it had a different intended meaning behind it. Uzma Maroof, 'The Two Nation Theory: The Myth, The Reality', available in http://www.storyofpakistan.com/contribute.asp?artid=co31&pd-1 (last accessed on 02/28110).

23. 'Hindu Nationalism', available in http://www.search.com/reference/Hindu-nationalism (last accessed on 05117/10).
24. 'Hindu Origins of Two Nation Theory', available in http://defence.pk/forums/world-affairs/19429-hindu-origins-twi-nations-theory.html (last accessed on 05/17/10).
25. In the provincial election of 1946 the Muslim League got 93 per cent of Muslim votes in the province and 119 out of 250 in the Assembly. See more in Sekhar Bandyopadhya, *op. cit.*, pp. 446–447.
26. *Ibid.*, pp. 443–444.
27. The Cabinet Mission Plan rejected the proposal of a sovereign Pakistan with six provinces and offered a loose federal government for the Union of India including both provinces and princely states. *Ibid.*, pp. 449–451.
28. The Breakdown Plan was, in the case of disagreement the British will withdraw from the six provinces of Pakistan, and the Congress would deal with the rest of India. *Ibid.*, p. 454.

29. According to Plan Balkan the partition of Punjab and Bengal and handing over of power to the provinces and sub-provinces would be decided on the basis of self-determination and an Interim Government would remain till June 1948. *Ibid.,* pp. 454–455.

30. Salient features of Lord Mountbatten Plan were: (paraphrased as):

    1. There should be two sovereign states in India, the Central government of each state should take over power in responsibility to their respective Constituent Assembly, on dominion state basis.
    2. The transfer of power in either case should be on the basis of the Government of India Act 1935.
    3. The Governor-General should be common to both the dominions.
    4. A commission should be appointed for demarcation of boundaries in the event of decision in favour of partition.

    The features were designed in such a way that before 14th August 1947, it was in 3rd June 1947, (where the plan was brought out) India was divided into India and Pakistan, available in http://www.indianetzone.com/42/mountbatten_plan.htm (last accessed on *02/28/10).*

31. Banglapedia: *'Nationalism',* National Encyclopaedia of Bangladesh, Islamabad, 2006.

32. Abdus Sattar Ghazali, *Islamic Pakistan: Illusions and Reality,* National Book Club, Islamabad, 2006.

33. G.W. Choudhury, 'Bangladesh Why it Happened?' *International Affairs,* Vol. 48, No. 2, April 1972, pp. 242–249.

34. *Ibid.,* p. 242.

35. Failure of Pakistan to Develop A Political System CSS Forum', available in http://www.cssforum.com/lok/css-compulsory-subjects/pakistan-affairs/4651-failure-

Pakistan-develop-politicalsyatem.htm (last accessed on 05/15/10).

36. G.W. Choudhury, *op. cit.,* p. 242.
37. *Ibid.,* pp. 242–243
38. The politicians of West Pakistan were feudal lords while East Pakistan had urbanised politicians. Therefore, there was always a clash over the idea of whether Pakistan should have a rural dominated political base or urbanised dominated one. After the creation of Pakistan Jinnah himself concentrated maximum power in his hands which led to the rise of discontentment among, the political leaders of East Pakistan. The failure of parliamentary democracy was mainly responsible for the rise of a powerful bureaucracy and military. See more in 'Failure of Pakistan to Develop A Political System CSS Forum', available in http://www.cssforum.com/ok/css-compulsory-subjects/pakistan-affairs/4651-failure-Pakistan-develop-politicalsyatem.htm (last accessed on 05/15/10).
39. Pakistan had her first Constitution 1956.
40. East Pakistan was of the opinion that the concentration of power in a Presidential system was in favour of West Pakistan whereas parliamentary democracy would be better solution for the distribution of power. But on the contrary West Pakistan the feudallords were not ready to share their political power with the people of East Pakistan. Therefore, ultimately there was no balance between political representations of both the wings of Pakistan. See more in 'Failure of Pakistan to Develop A Political System CSS Forum', available in http://www.cssforum.com/ok/css-compulsory-subjects/pakistan-affairs/4651-failure-Pakistan-develop- politicalsyatem.htm (last accessed on 05/15/10).
41. The West Pakistani officials considered themselves superior therefore they never bothered about the presence of Bengali Muslim's of East Pakistan. Thus, it resulted in bitterness and widening of gap between these two groups of people. G.W. Choudhury, *op. cit.,* pp. 242–244.

42. Salahuddin Ahmed, *Bangladesh: Past and Present,* A.B.H. Publishers, New Delhi, 2004, p. 157.
43. *Ibid.,* pp. 174-176 .
44. *Ibid.,* pp. 158–160.
45. Sumit Ganguly, *op. cit.,* pp. 47–53 .
46. *Ibid.,* p. 54.
47. In the Agartala Conspiracy case the Central government of Pakistan arrested 35 persons in 1968 for allegedly engaging in a conspiracy to bring about the secession of East Pakistan with the help of India. Sheikh Mujibur Rahamn was arrested on the same charge (but the fact is it was a plan to undermine the growing image of Mujibur among the people of East Pakistan). Salahuddin Ahmed, *op. cit.,* pp. 161–163.
48. 'Bangladesh Liberation War', available in http://en.wikipedia.org/wiki/Bangladesh liberation war (last accesssed on 02/11/10).
49. 'Bangladesh Liberation War', available in http://en.wikipedia.org/wiki/Bangladesh liberation war (last accesssed on 02/11/10).
50. Sirajullslam, *History of Bangladesh: 1704-1971, Economic History,* Asiatic Society of Bangladesh, Dhaka, 1992.
51. G.W. Choudhury, *op. cit.,* pp. 242–249.
52. *Ibid.,* pp. 245–246.
53. *Ibid* p. 246.
54. Sirajul Islam, *History of Bangladesh: 1704–1971. Economic History. op. cit.*, pp. 777–780.
55. See details in Salahuddin Ahmed, *op. cit.,*p. 137 and Sirajul Islam, *History of Bangladesh: 1704–1971. Cultural History,* Asiatic Society of Bangladesh, Dhaka, 1992, p. 803.
56. Salahuddin Ahmed, *op. cit.,* p. 137.
57. *Ekushe* February is written in golden letters in the history of Bangladesh and it is observed with full respect and dignity.

58. Dr. Mohammad Sahidulha's idea quoted from Ashad Choudhury, *Bangladesher Mukti Juddhho,* Bangla Academy, Dhaka, 1983.
59. M. Niaz Asadullah, *'Educational Disparities in Pakistan:* 1947–1971 (presentation paper of UK Economic and Social History Conference), 2004.
60. *Ibid.,* pp. 4–5.
61. *Ibid.,* p. 5.
62. Pakistan: Civil-Military Relationship Praetorian State', available in http://epress.anv.mdap/mobile_ devices/ ch06.html (last accessed on *03/17/10)* and 'Civil Military Relations', available in http://civilmilltaryrelat10 nshipcontemporarypakistan_ihtm (last accessed on *03/17/10).*
63. Parity of Representation: East Pakistan's Bengalis wanted to use their majority strength in the Assembly but this was denied in the name of parity of representation for the two units. Therefore, East Pakistan's numerical majority was artificially proportionate with the numbers of West Pakistan as the Punjabis of West Pakistan were not ready to accept the majority dominance of East Pakistan. In reality there was no parity of representation. See M. Rafiqul Islam. *International Legal Implications: The Bangladesh Liberation Movement*, UPL, Dhaka, 1987, p. 16.
64. One Unit Bill- as East Pakistan was one united large province vis-a-vis the four distributed provinces of West Pakistan. Therefore, the Punjabis of West Pakistan wanted integration of all four to establish their dominance over East Pakistan. This proposal was forcefully rejected by the majority of East Pakistani, but this rejection did not succeed. Rather the Constituent Assembly was dissolved and in 1955 Iskander Mirza amended the 1935 Government of India Act, and he merged all the provinces of the West into one and declared one Constitution for all the provinces of Pakistan. *Ibid.,* pp. 16–18.

65. Pakistan: Civil-Military Relationship Praetorian State', available in http://epress.anv.mdap/mobile devices/ ch06.html(last accessed on 03/17/10) and 'Civil Military Relations', available in http://civllmilitaryrelatlonshipcon temporarypakistan_1htm (last accessed on 03/17/10).
66. Salahuddin Ahmed, *op. cit.,* p. 168.
67. *Ibid.,* pp. 168–169 and see 'Bangladesh Liberation War', available in http://en.wikipedia.org/wiki Bnagladesh_ liberation_war (last accessed on 02/11/10).
68. See Dr Syed Ehtisham, 'Pakistan, Bangladesh and Stateless People', available in http://www.thesouthasian. org/archives/2004/Pakistan_bangladesh_and_theSt.htm l(last accessed on 04/14/10).
69. Salahuddin Ahmed, *op. cit.,* p. 177.
70. The words of official declaration was:-*Today Bangladesh is a sovereign country and independent country ... The Bengalis are fighting the enemy (West Pakistan Army) with great courage for an independent Bangladesh. May Allah aid us in our fight for freedom. Joy Bangla,* available in http://www.wikipedia.org/wiki/Bangladesh_Liberation_ War (last accessed on 02/22/10).
71. Salahuddin Ahmed, *op. cit.,* p. 201.
72. Syed Nazrul Islam as the president of Bangladesh, Tafuddin Ahmed as Prime Minister, Khondhar Mushtaque Ahmed as the Minister of Foreign Affairs and Law and Parliamentary Affairs. *Ibid.,* p. 202.
73. Mukti Bahini was an armed organisation that fought alongside with Indian Armed Force against the Pakistan Army during Bangladesh Liberation War in 1971. It was formed by civilians and regulars of Bangladesh and it was joined by the former members of East Pakistan Armed Force, available in http://en.wikipedia.org/wiki/Mukti–Bahini, (last accessed on 03/01/10).
74. Salahuddin Ahmed, *op. cit.,* p. 203.
75. See details in 'Involvement in Bangladesh Liberation War', available in http://www.shvoong.com/humanities/1708532-

involvement-bangladesh-liberation-war (last accessed on 03/01/10).

76. Following were strategies adopted by Mukti Bahini against the West Pakistan Army:
    1. A large number of guerrillas were sent inside Bangladesh to carry out raids and ambushes.
    2. Industries were brought out to standstill and electricity supply were disrupted.
    3. Pakistanis were obstructed in exporting manufactured goods and raw materials.
    4. Communication networks were destroyed to obstruct every movement. See more in http://en.wikipedia.org/wild/Mukti_Bahini (last accessed on 03/01/10).

77. The eleven sectors of Bangladesh Liberation war were: 1. Chittagong District, Chittagong Hill Tracts, and the entire eastern area of the Noakhali district on the banks of the river Muhuri, The headquarters of the sector was at Harina. Chittagong district, Chittagong Hill Tracts, and the entire eastern area of the Noakhali district on the banks of the river Muhuri. The headquarters of the sector was at Harina. 2. Districts of Dhaka, Com in a, and Faridpur, and part of Noakhali district. 3. Area between Churaman Kathi (near Sreemangal) and Sylhetin the north and Singerbil of Brahmanbariain the south. 4. Area from Habiganj district on the north to Kanaighat Police Station on the south along the 100 mile long border with India. The headquarters of the sector was initially at Karimganj and later at Masimpur. 5. Area from Durgapur to Danki (Tamabil) of Sylhet district and the entire area up to the eastern borders of the district. The headquarters of the sector was at Banshtala. 6. Rangpur district and part of Dinajpur district. The headquarters of the sector was at Burimari near Patgram. 7. Rajshahi, Pabna, Bograand part of Dinajpur district. The headquarters of the sector was at Taranngapur. 8. In April 1971, the operational area of the sector comprised the districts of Kushtia, Jessore, Khulna, Barisal, Faridpurand

Patuakhali. At the end of May, the sector was reconstituted and comprised the districts of Kuhstia, Jessore, Khulna, Satkhira and the northern part of Faridpur district. The headquarters of the sector was at Benapole. 9. Barisal, Patuakhali, and parts of the district of Khulna and Faridpur. 10. This sector was constituted with the naval commandos. 11. Mymen Singh and Tangail along with parts of Rangpur-Gaibandha, Ulipur, Kamalpur and Chilmari. The headquarters of the sector was at Teldhala until October 10, then transferred to Mahendraganj.

78. Lawrence Lifschultz, *Bangladesh: The Unfinished Revolution,* Zed Press, London, 1979, p. 21.

79. *Ibid.,* pp. 21–22.

80. *Ibid.,* pp. 21–23.

81. On 23rd October 1971, President Yahya Khan declared the proclamation of state of emergency by saying "a most critical situation has been created because Pakistan is faced with external aggression". Salahuddin Ahmed, *op. cit.,* p. 203.

82. *Ibid.,* pp. 203–204.

83. The reason behind USA's supported to West Pakistan Army was that, USA wanted to have good relation with China, so that she can have a strong support vis-a-vis USSR. With USA's involvement in the war, the world was witnessing clash between the then super powers USA and USSR.

84. US send Task Force 74 of Seven Fleet in Bay of Bengal during the last phase of Bangladesh Liberation War. Task Force 74 comprised nuclear-powered air craft. Destroyers, nuclear-powered attack submarine, supply shifts. This Task Force reached on 14th December 1971, but on 16th December 1971, West Pakistan Government surrendered. See details in 'United States 7th Fleet' available in http://en.wikipedia.orglwiki/United-States Fleet (last accessed on 3/11/10) and Salahuddin Ahmed, *op. cit.,* pp. 203–204.

85. Salahuddin Ahmed, *op. cit.,* pp. 205–206.

86. M. Rafiqul Islam, *op. cit.,* pp. 30–32.

87. *Ibid.,* p. 38.
88. *Ibid.,* p. 40.
89. *Ibid.,* p. 41.
90. *Ibid.,* p. 127.
91. Human Rights are international moral and legal norms that aspire to protect all people everywhere from severe political, legal and social abuses. The main source of the contemporary conception of Human Rights is the Universal Declaration of Human Rights (1948). The internationally recognised Human Rights fall into the following categories:
    1. Rights of a person refers to life, liberty and security of the person, privacy and freedom of movement, ownership of property, freedom of thought, religion and conscience and prohibition of slavery, torture and cruel or degrading punishment.
    2. Rights associated with rule of law including equal recognition before the law and equal protection of the law, effective legal remedy for violation of legal rights, prohibition of arbitrary arrest.
    3. Political rights include freedom of expression, assembly and association, right to take part in government and periodic and general elections by universal and equal suffrage.
    4. Economic and social rights refer to an adequate standard of living, free choice of employment, protection against unemployment, reasonable limitations of working hours, free elementary education, social security etc.
    5. Rights of communities include self-determination and protection of minority activities. See more in Amal Ray and Mohit Bhattacharya, *Political Theory: Ideas and Institutions,* World Press, India, 2003, pp. 195–196 and Rajeev Bhargava and Ashok Acharya, *Political Theory: An Introduction,* Pearson, New Delhi, 2010, pp. 98–99.
92. M. Rafiqul Islam, *op. cit.*, pp. 156–158 and Rudi Gurazin,

'Is Humanitarian Military Intervention in the Affairs of Another State Ever Justified?', *Global Political Security* and *International Studies Middlesex University,* 2008, pp. 3–4.

93. Rudi Gurazin, *op. cit.,* p. 4.
94. *Ibid.,* pp. 3–4.
95. Non-interventionist is base on the idea that a state should not interfere 'in the international politics of another state-based upon the principles of state sovereignty and self-determination, available in http://en.wikipedia.ogr/wiki/Non-Intervention (last accessed on 04/03/10).
96. Restrictionist belief in putting restriction on the activities of the state.
97. Rudi Gurazin, *op. cit.,* p. 4.
98. The Indian Ambassador at the UN argued that, the "military repression" in East Pakistan was on a sufficient scale to "shock the conscience of mentioned", *ibid.,* pp. 7–8.
99. C.A.J. Coady, 'War and Intervention', in Catriona Mckinnon, *Issues in Political Theory,* Oxford University Press, New York, 2008.
100. *Ibid.,* p. 65.
101. *Ibid.,* pp. 58–59.
102. M. Rafiqul Islam, *op. cit.,* p. 157.
103. *Ibid.,* p. 265.
104. *Ibid.,* pp. 265–266.
105. *Ibid.,* pp. 266–272.
106. *Ibid.,* p. 271.
107. Salahuddin Ahmed, *op. cit.,* p. 207.
108. *Ibid.,* p. 207–208.

3

Government and Governance of Bangladesh

In the first chapter, it began with the distinction present between the theory and practice of the Right to self-determination and secession. According to the theory of both these concepts, people of a given territory demand a Right to self-determination and secession when they lack participation in the government and governance of their country. By following this theoretical perspective in the second chapter, it discussed on one case of secession that is East Pakistan's secession from West Pakistan which led to the birth of Bangladesh in 1971. In the East Pakistan case, it was lack of participation which became the guiding force for demanding secession from West Pakistan. Therefore, it is clear that demands for secession arise when a group of people are constantly denied their equal status vis-a-vis the rest of the people of the country. This discrimination leads to lack of participation in political, social, economic, cultural space for a particular group of people. Thus, it is very important to have a balanced relationship between people and government of a country in order to avoid the extreme situation (secession).

In this chapter, the primary focus is to analyse the governance structure of Bangladesh. These analyses would help not only to understand the political structure of Bangladesh but it would also help to understand how democratic and participatory is Bangladesh at present, because Bangladesh herself was a victim of non-democratic and non-participatory government structure in unified Pakistan (from 1947 to 1971).

Governmental Transitions and Regime Change in Bangladesh: From Independence to the Present

The independence of Bangladesh in 1971 was a negation of Jinnah's Two Nation Theory, according to which Hindus and Muslims are two distinct nations and therefore they should be entitled to two separate and sovereign states.[1] But this belief could not last for a longer period of time (see Chapter 2), because of the military dictatorship of West Pakistan over East Pakistan. Thus, when Bangladesh got her independence and framed the Constitution in 1972 (Fig 3.1), Mujibur Rahman declared Bangladesh as the Peoples' Republic of Bangladesh and pledged to uphold nationalism, secularity, democracy and socialism. The Constitution also ensures its citizens—the rule of law, fundamental human rights and freedoms as well as equality and justice, political, economic and social.[2] All these commitments made the Constitution of Bangladesh a democratic one. The 1972 Constitution of Bangladesh followed the pattern of Britain and the United States by granting human rights and political freedoms within the system of checks and balances.[3] With all these options, freedoms and facilities Mujibur promised his fellow countrymen "*Sonar Bangla*" (Golden Bengal).[4] But within a short span of time Bangladesh witnessed too many problems like the task of rebuilding the country, shortfall in domestic production, abnormal rise in the prices of essential commodities (rice, sugar, edible oil, cloths etc.), while the government of the country succumbed to red tapism and corruption.[5] Though, it is true that after winning the 1973 elections the Awami League tried hard to resolve these problems but the situation always remained difficult.[6] In this background, Mohammadullah (the then President of Bangladesh) declared a state of emergency in

Fig. 3.1. Political Map of Bangladesh.

1974, and this led to the suspension of all fundamental rights guaranteed under the Constitution.[7] In less than a month, Mujibur on 25th January 1975, against the wishes of the Parliament, amended the Constitution shifting from a parliamentary to a presidential form of government.[8] He was authorised to form one National Party. Thus, he formed Bangladesh Krishak Sramik Awami League (BKSAL) and simultaneously suspended all other political parties. The amendment also declared Mujibur as the President of Bangladesh for five years from the date of the Constitutional amendment.[9] On 6th June 1975, Mujibur announced the Constitution of BKSAL and also nominated the members of Executive Committee and Central Committee[10] and appealed to all other political parties to join under this national party but despite his appeal many political parties refused to join the national party.[11] The formation of BKSAL led to:

- The rise of authoritarian leadership.
- The press was put under the control of the government except for *Bangladesh Observer* and *Dainik Bangla.*[12]
- Though, in order to overcome the deteriorating political and economic situation Mujibur announced a new system of local administration yet he himself controlled the districts and their governors.[13]
- Mujibur's regime presented the people authoritarianism in the name of democracy, social injustice in the name of socialism, national disunity in the name of Bengali nationalism and communal disharmony in the name of secularism.[14]

All these resulted in growing hatred towards Mujibur's regime, because throughout the Bangladesh liberation war he strongly advocated the ideals of a parliamentary system of democratic governance against the presidential form of rule of Pakistan. But after the independence of Bangladesh he himself followed the course of presidential rule in the name of overcoming the fast deteriorating condition of

Bangladesh.[15] But this step of Mujibur proved very costly for him because the majority of the population was against the change. One more thing which negatively affected Mujibur was his neglected attitude towards the jawans and military (except Jatio Rakkhi Bahini, JRB).[16] According to Muhammad Yeahia Akhter[17] this failure of Mujibur to control the corruption, smuggling, secret killings, rise of other military groups introduction of one party rule, etc., ultimately led to the formation of the August 15 Coup of 1975.[18] This bloody coup made simultaneous attacks on the residences of Mujibur, Sheikh Moni and Abdur Rab Sarinabad which led to the end of "Sheikh dynasty"[19] (except Sheikh Hasina, because she was out of Bangladesh). This coup surrounded the JRB headquarters. After this, Khondokhar Mushtaq Ahmed (the foreign trade minister of Mujibur's cabinet) declared himself as the President of Bangladesh. The new President made the following changes[20]:

- Major General Ziaur Rahman (Zia) was appointed as the chief of the army staff.
- Politicians who were arrested under Mujibur's regime were released.
- Newspapers which were put under governmental check got their status back.
- The proposal of administrative decentralisation was kept aside for further review.
- The one party system was abolished and the formation of BKSAL was declared as null and void.

Mushtaque not only brought about these internal changes, he also made a significant change in foreign policy, as he sent a letter to Bhutto which offered to normalise Bangladesh's relation with Pakistan.[21] But while Mushtaque was busy trying to control the situation in Bangladesh with the help of his military, a second coup brought an immediate end to his regime on 3rd November

1975. This new coup was led by Brigadier Khaled Musharraf. This military coup put Ziaur Rahman under house arrest and Musharraf declared himself as the chief of the army and made the then Chief Justice of the Bangladesh A.S.M. Sayem the President of Bangladesh.[22] But this military coup could not last for more than four days because another military coup led by Colonel Abu Taher named as the "Sepoy Mutiny" killed Musharraf and again brought Zia into power.[23] After Zia came into power he primarily faced challenged from the pro-Mujib forces and from the Leftist guerrilla forces under the leadership of Abu Taher. Therefore, Zia ordered the arrest of Taher and finally he executed him in a secret trial in a military court.[24] However, because of Zia's anti-Mujib attitude he suspected India's involvement in Bangladesh, as he was of the opinion that India had a pro-Mujib attitude thereby affecting his prospects. Thus, he was skeptical of India's intentions and sought to move closer to the Western and Islamic world while maintaining a distanced from India.[25]

Zia was the first military ruler of independent Bangladesh. From 1975 to 1977 he worked as the army chief, but in April 1977 he gave a speech that on 30th May 1977 a referendum would be held, to get the confidence of Bangladeshis, to make him the President of Bangladesh.[26] Accordingly a referendum was held on the said day and the result was overwhelming support for Zia's Presidentship. As soon as he became the President of Bangladesh, he declared a 19-point programme for addressing the impoverishment of the nation and he was taking care to reduce corruption also.[27] Zia's presidentship was marked by the constitutional changes taken by him. He replaced the one party system with a multi-party system; socialism was redefined as economic and social justice; Bengali nationalism was replaced by Bangladeshi nationalism while the most significant change was the replacement of the term secularism with "absolute faith in the almighty Allah". Zia brought about the 15th constitutional amendment and added *Bismillahir Rahmanir Rahim* (in the name of Allah, the beneficent, the merciful).[28] By replacing the three basic principles of the Constitution he virtually changed the nature of Bangladesh's polity and the replacement of the term secular with the sanctification of an Islamic state was a major blow to the struggle, which the people of Bangladesh fought during their liberation war. After all, the root cause for the birth of Bangladesh was the extreme discrimination, cultural and political against Bengalis.

The Presidential election of 1978 consolidated Zia's position and in 1979 after a long period, parliamentary elections were held which put an end to martial rule and the emergency situation. All these major achievements helped him in strengthening his political party, the Bangladesh Nationalist Party (BNP). Though, initially Zia's Islam-based political discourse legitimised his power and he got support from the people yet after some time this support was restricted to the International Islamic world and he lost the support of his fellow countrymen. Rather he faced the challenge of the rise of two distinct type of ideologies—Islam and secularism. And moreover these two distinct terms became the splitting factor of Bangladesh on the question of identity politics.

Zia not only made constitutional changes he also carried out some developmental activities. So, his 19-point programme dealt with the socio-economic development of the country and he also undertook a rural mobilisation programme.[29] Zia very cleverly appointed the members of BNP, as he chose people from all types of background[30] which helped him in splitting his major oppositions. All these initiatives of Zia indicate that he was quite efficient in his military rule. But despite his efforts he was assassinated in another military coup on 31st May 1981. After the assassination of Zia, Abdus Sattar became the acting President of the country. Though, he got victory in the presidential election of 1981 as a BNP candidate, his regime lasted for four months only because he was neither able to satisfy the army nor was he able to maintain political stability in the country.[31]

After the failure of Sattar's regime, Bangladesh came under military leadership. On 24th March 1982, the Army Chief, Lieutenant General Hussain Muhammad Ershad took control of the government through the military coup.[32] He first declared martial law in the country and then he suspended the Constitution, disbanded the Parliament, deprived the President, Prime Minister and Cabinet Ministers of their offices.[33] Initially, he became the Chief Minister of the new Cabinet and Supreme Court Justice Abdul Fazal Muhammad Ahsanuddin Chowdhury became the interim President. But later on in December 1983, Ershad himself became the President of Bangladesh. Though, he made a declaration that he will try to establish democratic rule yet the polity under him always witnessed martial law and those who opposed martial law were imprisoned for seven years.[34]

After establishing control, Ershad had primarily three objectives.[35]

- To act against corruption and reorganise the administrative apparatus.
- To stand as a strong centralising force while keeping his civilian opponents at a distance.
- To assuage and control the military to avoid any further military coups.

Working on these objectives he tried to follow the steps of the former military ruler Zia. Therefore, he first brought a reform programme into local government. Though, it seems that his primary focus was on the process of decentralisation (creation of a new administrative unit *upazila)*, yet in real terms he was not interested in introducing a participatory model of governance but wanted to use the *upazila* for fulfilling his own political interests.[36] To avoid the formation of further military coups, Ershad granted huge funds to the military and also appointed high army personnel in the administration of the country.[37] This tendency of militarisation of the administration created a problem as it was not accepted by the bureaucrats. Thus, a tussle between the military and the civilian bureaucracy began under his regime. Ershad like Zia also brought out socio-economic development programmes, and thus he offered an 18-point programme. Simultaneously, he worked for the protection and flourishing of private capital and promoted a privatisation process. But despite these steps opposition to his military rule emerged.

In 1983, a 15-party alliance, led by the Awami League under the leadership of Sheikh Hasina Wajed and a seven party alliance led by BNP under the leadership of Begum Khaleda Zia and some other parties came together and called for the "Movement for Restoration of Peace".[38] Though, it is true that the Awami League and BNP were not and are still not united on constitutional issues yet both of them believed that military rule should be withdrawn and power transferred to a civilian government established through peaceful and free and fair elections based on a parliamentary system. As a result of this opposition, Sheikh Hasina and Khaleda Zia were arrested, but still the opposition leaders were not ready to cooperate with martial law rule. Thus, violence and civil disobedience prevailed in the country. Then Ershad decided to have a political dialogue with the opposition parties but the opposition parties were not ready for this. Then in 1985, he organised a "civilisation" programme without the participation of the opposing parties and also arranged a referendum to have a clear opinion about him by the people of Bangladesh.[39]

The result of the referendum was in his favour but according to other parties the result was manipulated. After the referendum Ershad released Sheikh Hasina and

Khaleda Zia and also declared that he would hold a parliamentary election and after that a presidential election. Despite his declaration the BNP boycotted the parliamentary election but he got the participation of Awami League and the 15-party alliance.[40] Despite BNP's absence Ershad moved ahead and summoned the Parliament to discuss the [41]amendment to the Constitution which would ratify his power over Bangladesh and also justify his implementation of martial law. But this step proved very costly for him because neither the people of Bangladesh nor the opposition political parties were ready to compromise on his terms and thus the opposition political parties boycotted the sessions of Parliament," and also made a demand for the resignation of Ershad.

Even as there was this political turmoil the country witnessed extensive flooding which created much misery in the country especially as governmental relief efforts were not at all adequate. The opposing parties jointly came out into the streets of Bangladesh against the Ershad regime.[42] In the background of this joint opposition, Ershad dissolved the Parliament and declared a fresh election in 1988. Accordingly, the election was held but the Awami League, BNP and other parties boycotted it. This particular action of the opposition made it clear that the Ershad style of politics was not acceptable. Then Ershad did another blunder by bringing out the 8th Constitutional amendment, according to which Islam was declared as the state religion.[43] Through this he wanted to win the confidence of the Muslim population but the irony was that the majority of the population was against this amendment. The BNP-Ied seven party alliance said that the parliamentary membership was illegally constituted and had no right to amend the Constitution. The Awami-League led eight-party alliance criticised the amendment as a unjustified move to destroy the sprit of the Bangladesh liberation struggle.[44] By 1990, Ershad came under severe pressure, when the All Party Student Unity (APSU), and other opposition alliances announced that they wanted the immediate resignation of Ershad and the formation of a Non-party Caretaker Government (NCG) under whom fresh parliamentary elections could be conducted.[45] All these actions forced Ershad to resign from his post and finally he handed over power to Shahabuddin Ahmed (the then Chief Justice of Supreme Court). This transfer of power led to the end of the second episode of military rule in Bangladesh.

After the end of military rule in 1990 parliamentary elections were held in 1991 under the NCG, which resulted in the emergence of the BNP as the ruling party and Khaleda Zia as Prime Minister. Awami League became the main opposition party under Sheikh Hasina.[46] As the first woman Prime Minister of Bangladesh Khaleda Zia passed the 12th constitutional amendment bill in the Parliament to reintroduce a parliamentary form of government in place of the presidential form of government.[47] Apart from amending the Constitution, she also brought about progress in the educational sectors, introduction of free and compulsory primary education and promoted certain social campaigns such as tree planting. Despite these steps, she faced pressure from the opposition to introduce measures in the Parliament to amend the Constitution to ensure the establishment of NCG to conduct future parliamentary elections.[48] The ruling party criticised the views of the opposition and thus a gap developed between the ruling party and the opposition. The opposition party suggested a proposal[49] for the formation of NCG, but the ruling party ignored the proposal by saying that it was against the provisions of the Constitution.

Like this, 21 more proposals were proposed but unfortunately they were all rejected either by the ruling party or by the opposition parties.[50] The disturbed political situation further detoriorated with the election result of Magura-2 constituency bye-election.[51] Though, the BNP candidate won the election and the election took place under Election Commission's guidance nonetheless the Awami League and other opposition parties alleged electoral fraud also declared that they would not participate in any elections under the BNP government. Because of this opposition Parliament was dissolved and the Election Commission declared that new parliamentary election would be held in February 1996. Again, in this election Khaleda Zia became the Prime Minister for a second time. But all major parties boycotted the election and again made a plea for the neutral formation of NCG. Thus, again Parliament was dissolved to conduct the next parliamentary election under a new NCG.

The 12th June, 1996 election gave a clear victory to the Awami League and made Sheikh Hasina the new Prime Minister of the People's Republic of Bangladesh. It was her party which gave the people of Bangladesh the chance to replace military rule.[52] Sheikh Hasina first secured the peoples right to vote freely and then work for the neutral establishment of a NCG.[53] Simultaneously, she carried out many economic, social and political reforms, like a poverty alleviation programme, creation of job opportunities, increase in food production, etc.[54] She had worked for the poorer sections of society even when she was in opposition.[55] Two other major achievements of Sheikh Hasina's period of rule were firstly, the Ganga Water Sharing Treaty signed between India and Bangladesh.[56] and secondly the signing of the Peace Accord with the tribal dissidents of Chittagong Hill Tracts.[57] Despite so many achievements, in the new millennium the Awami League witnessed a landslide defeat in the 2001 parliamentary elections and thus again the BNP-led four-party alliance emerged as the ruling force and Awami League became the opposition. But still the significant point was that for the first time a freely and fairly elected party had completed its five-year term.

This third tenure of the BNP as a ruling party and the Awami League as an opposition party witnessed more problems than previously. Rising political violence and religious militancy became a serious point of contention between them.[58] In this term, the BNP came closer to Jamaat-i-Islami (JP) an Islamic Party and to the Islamic Oikya Jote.[59] Therefore, the opposition party was of the opinion that again there was a possibility of the rise of Islamic fundamentalism. The law and order system was at stake because of the rise of murders, abductions, etc.[60] Given these activities, the government established speedy tribunals, formed a Rapid Action Team of Police, but the situation deteriorated further.[61] And it reached its peak when in 2004 a grenade attack was planned against Sheikh Hasina (the opposition party leader).[62] Meanwhile the country also witnessed a non-functional Parliament, as the main opposition party remained absent from the Parliament. Though, some reforms were made like an increase in the reservation of seats for women in Parliament, extension of retirement age of Supreme Court Judges,[63] yet the party could not win the heart of the opposition. Not only did the national policies taken by her affect her image, even foreign policy decisions taken by her also affected her status.[64] Thus, because of the unstable situation and the BNP government's failure to tackle the situation, the 2007 election were postponed and a state of emergency was imposed on Bangladesh.[65] In April 2007, the Bangladesh police declared that they would investigate extortion charges against Sheikh Hasina, and then she was charged with murder.[66] Thus, the government of Bangladesh ordered the airlines not to allow her to return to Dhaka as she was in United States at that time.[67] On 22nd April 2007, an arrest warrant was issued against her but she wanted to defend herself. Thus, on 23rd April 2007 the arrest warrant was suspended and on 25th April 2007 the ban on Sheikh Hasina's return to Bangladesh was also dropped.[68] On July 2007, Sheikh Hasina was arrested on extortion charges, but this arrest of Hasina became a political issue. Finally the extortion charges were suspended and she was released on parole for medical reasons on January 2008.[69] In November 2008, she returned to Bangladesh and announced her election manifesto. This time the Awami League came in as a ruling majority and the BNP became the opposition. The Awami League's victory in the election generated a new hope for Bangladesh, because the party declared that their primary aim would be to promote economic growth, to make Bangladesh free from terrorism, establish a democratic welfare state and pursue other developmental and progressive policies.[70] In her second tenure, Sheikh Hasina is looking into both national and international matters. She made an announcement that the "use of religion and communalism in politics will be banned" signalling her intent to protect the minorities.[71] In the international field she is presently working for improving her country's relations with the neighbouring countries.[72] If the party moves in this direction then there is a possibility that Bangladesh can move towards a more democratic and participatory polity.

Is the Governance System of Bangladesh Participatory in Nature?

One can recognise Bangladesh as a field of confrontational politics because of its inherent structural problems like the deteriorating state of law and order, administration, etc. As these problems are so embedded in the social and political life of the country, a doubt has arisen about the governance system of the country. A country's governance is about how its economical, political and administrative authorities maintain their affairs at all levels of the country.[73] Therefore, governance comprises the mechanisms, processes and institutions through which citizens and groups articulate their interests, exercise legal' rights, meet their obligations and mediate their differences.[74] The World Bank in its Governance and Development Report of 1992 says that a country's governance has three aspects[75]:

- The form of political regime (parliamentary or presidential, military or civilian and authoritarian or democratic).
- The process by which authority is exercised in the management of the country's economic and social resources.
- The capacity of the government to design, formulate and implement policies and in general to discharge governmental functions.

Keeping these guidelines in mind, it can be said that Bangladesh's polity is a mixture of military rule and parliamentary democracy. Up to and including the tenure of Ershad rule, the country witnessed military dominance over government (except between 1971 to 1973). Even after 1990, when parliamentary democracy was again put in place confrontational politics with the potential for bringing in military influence remained a worrying feature.

Present Features of Bangladesh Governance

1. The Shift from Military Regime to Bi-party System: Absence of a Multi-Party System

Bangladesh began its political journey with the idea of multi-party system, then it shifted to a one party system and now it has moved towards a two-party system or bi-party system after 1990. If we go by the democratic features of governance then the presence of a multi-party system is one of the primary requirements for its proper working. But in the case of Bangladesh, it had witnessed the dominance of military-based rule for such a long period of time that even the emergence of a bi-party system is a satisfactory achievement.

After the end of one-party military dominance, the Awami League and the BNP emerged as the two most dominant political parties of Bangladesh's polity. Such a bi-polar system is visualised as a point of stability for a country's polity, but in the case of Bangladesh this has became a point of constant conflict and confrontation, because voters do not have a wider option. Therefore, even the political parties are more interested in establishing their dominance than looking into the arguments of the opposition as they are aware of the fact that at one or the other time they would establish their dominance by becoming the ruling side.

In Bangladesh, the ruling party as a routine procedure never consults the opposition party. Rather it (the ruling party) considers its view point as that of the entire country. Therefore, the ruling party demonstrates a high degree of intolerance towards the political opposition.[76] This intolerance leads to the rise of confrontational politics as there is no cooperation, trust and solidarities among the political parties. The ruling and opposition parties do not have any consensus on national and international issues.[77] Therefore, rather than offering a strong ruling party and opposition party, the Bangladesh polity produce a very weak and fragile two-party system where the opposition party opposes the ruling party merely for the sake of opposition, demanding that the ruling party should vacate office despite having an established majority in the parliament.[78]

2. Partial Working of Parliament

The first elected government of Bangladesh chose a parliamentary rather than a presidential form of government. But unfortunately the polity of Bangladesh could not retain the parliamentary form of government firstly because of the coming of military rule and secondly even after the end of military rule none of the political parties were ready to follow the principles of behaviour of a parliamentary form of government. In a parliamentary democracy both the ruling and the opposition party has a role to play. But in Bangladesh's parliamentary democracy when a party is in a ruling position then the opposition party boycotts the parliamentary sessions most of the time. That means in Bangladesh the opposition party does not perform its duties and responsibilities. The boycott of the Parliament by the opposition is adversely affecting the democratic progress of Bangladesh, as in the absence of the opposition in Parliament there is no one to voice the demand and aspiration of people and also to check the ruling party. The ruling party is effectively allowed to act arbitrarily.[79] This disrupts mainstream political life and prevents the development of democratic form of governance.[80] By boycotting the sessions of Parliament the opposition party deprives the constituents they represent of their voice in the House.[81]

This attitude of boycotting the works of Parliament also affects the working of Parliamentary Committees (PC), because the PCs also suffer from the pressure of the ruling parties. Thus, it leads to the rise of a less accountable and less transparent system and also contributes to the practice of mal=governance.[82]

3. Criminalisation of Politics: Role of Money and Power

The polity of Bangladesh witnessed perennial instability because the political leaders sought to gain power by adopting any type of means. This led to the use of extra-legal methods to achieve power. This gave rise to the coming of musclemen, *mastaans* in politics, and ultimately led to criminalisation of politics.[83] Therefore, many politicians of Bangladesh use *mastaans* as a political resource in order to achieve political office and access public resources for patronage purposes.

Under military rule one can expect "criminalisation of politics" for the motive of capturing the power, but in Bangladesh the same trend is present under civilian governments as well. The two major political parties use undemocratic means/instruments for fulfilling their electoral ambitions. Thus, both the political parties have abused the system of law enforcement and also institutionalised anarchy against fellow citizens of the country by favouring the *mastaans*.[84] Therefore, the main problem is that the political parties are losing their faith in the institution of free and fair methods for gaining position.

The coming of *mastaans* is an indication that in Bangladesh, money power plays an important role in the electoral procedure. Thus, elections have become a costly affair. In Bangladesh there is a lack of transparency especially with respect to matters of political financing and existing laws are inadequate for promoting of such transparency.[85] The commercialisation of politics reached its height when businessmen and black-money holders joined politics or when the politicians turned into businessmen. The pursuit of personal interests not public ones became their primary motivation.[86]

All these illegal and immoral activities show that in Bangladesh the judiciary is not fully independent.[87] But for the successful working of democracy independence of judiciary is essential, since the judiciary is not only the custodian of the Constitution but it is also the guarantor of people's fundamental rights and it is also responsible for the enforcement of good governance. Though, after the fall of Ershad the political parties called for the establishment of independent judiciary yet in practice it is not so. For example, the services of district and session judge, their transfer, promotion are controlled by the law ministry not by the Supreme Court. Therefore, a demand for transparency in the appointment of judges has been made to avoid partisan politics.[88] Because of this partisan politics, criminalisation of politics and a non-independent judiciary the country also suffers from the absence of rule of law. And good governance is the extension of rule of law, in whose absence, democratic governance is withering away.

4. Electoral Crisis

A democratic form of government is that in which the citizens are free to choose anyone. That means one of the basic requisites for the functioning of democracy are 'free and fair elections", so that all political parties have equal opportunities. Thus, election is the mechanism which selects and replaces the ruling party by providing a regular and systematic succession of government.[89] That means a country's political system can map the presence of democracy through its process of electoral operations. In the case of Bangladesh the idea of free and fair election was neither available under the military rule of Zia and Ershad nor is it available under the civilian rule of Khaleda Zia and Shiekh Hasina, because electoral corruption is a common feature of military rule as well as of civilian rule. One of the main similarities between Pakistan and Bangladesh is that they both practiced electoral corruption.

Electoral corruption means the rise of political and administrative immorality. Like Pakistan, in Bangladesh the process of democratisation has been hampered by the coming of military rule.[90] Military rulers have in practice manipulated the electoral process for establishing their control. But the irony is that civilian rule in Bangladesh also manipulated the electoral process.[91] The ruling party activists under the civilian rule in many places intimidated opposition candidates and institutionalised violence in collaboration with the administration. It is this lack of morality among the politicians that gave the idea of a special provision for the formation of NCG, instead a political government to arrange national elections.[92] NCG is the solution adopted by the people of Bangladesh because neither the military nor the civilian regime have conducted free and fair elections.

The formation of the NCG was a result of prolonged discussion among the ruling party and opposition party leaders. Because neither the party of military rule nor the party of civilian rule[93] was ready for its formation, they only agreed after tremendous pressure from a united opposition. In Bangladesh even the formation of NCG has not stopped electoral corruption because since independence press and media has been used as a mouthpiece of the ruling party.[94] Press and media were totally under the control of government under military rule. Though, this pressure is reduced under civilian rule yet the fact is that media freedom remains constrained.

5. Administrative Inefficiencies

The political system of Bangladesh has survived serious transitions. In 1990, when for the first time Bangladesh achieved a fully functional democracy after fifteen years of military rule, the nature and role of bureaucracy in both pre and post-democratic period remained almost the same with very few changes.[95] The two main problems of Bangladesh's bureaucratic structures are:

(a) Defective Recruitment Procedure: After the independence of Bangladesh, equal opportunities for all have become the basic principle of public service recruitment. However, there is a reserved quota for the entry of disadvantaged people. Despite these provisions, the recruitment procedure *per se* is not neutral. There are repeated instances of leakage of question papers and favouritism.[96] All these lead to complete failure of accountability and the absence of transparency. Even the Public Service Commission (PSC) has not been able to overcome such failures which are reported at every stage of preliminary and written examinations. As a result, large numbers of incompetent candidates are joining the service which in the long-run negatively affected the country 'creating' a weak, partisan and inefficient bureaucracy.[97]

Another problem of public service recruitment is the inadequate pay structures, which does not reward performance but favours personal relationships.[98] Therefore, the administration of Bangladesh suffers from politicisation of recruitment and advancement.

(b) Politicisation of Civil Services: Assassination of leaders, coups and counter-coups disturbed the polity of

Bangladesh and also increased the trend of political parties exercising undue influence on the bureaucracy. Under the military regime, the military rule and civil bureaucrats supported each other to secure their own positions. After 1990, when a parliamentary-democratic system of government was established for first time, the autonomy of the bureaucracy was challenged, which resulted in politicisation of bureaucracy, as the political parties recruited party men as bureaucrats, irrespective of their qualifications.[99]

Bangladesh's bureaucracy is so much under the influence of political parties that it has ignored the rules and regulations prescribed for civil servants.[100] The civil servants also started participating in the campaigning of political parties and some even stood in the elections with the support of the political parties.[101]

Governance in Bangladesh and the Issue of Human Development

In chapter 1, it was discussed that both economic growth and development are the indicators of progress. Therefore, improvement in economic conditions and reduction in poverty are not sufficient. The important aspect of human development, "which is a process of enlarging the range of people's choice—increasing their opportunities for education, health-care, income and employment and covering full range of human choices from a sound physical environment to economic and political freedom,[102] remained on the back burner or was neglected or relegated. According to the definition of human development, in order to measure the progress of a country, then one has to move beyond the single criteria of GNP[103], because human development is more about people, their development and enlarging their choices. It is true that economic growth, increased international trade and investment, technological advance are important but they are just means and people are the end.[104] The United Nations Development Programme

(UNDP) in 1990 brought about a report that elaborated what is known as the Human Development Index (HDI) to make an endeavour in this direction by declaring *Longevity, Knowledge* and *Decent Living Standard* as the basic elements of human life[105].

The year 1990 has its own significance as a new idea of human development (i.e., going beyond income) came into being. It is true that HDI which measures human development does not include all the parameters of human development (gender, income inequality, respect for human rights and political freedoms). But through its three parameters, HDI enables people to realise the relationship present between income and well-being.[106] For example, *Longevity*-gives people the right to life, *Knowledge*—gives people the scope to enlighten themselves so that they can understand the realities in a better way and finally, *Decent Living Standard*-gives people the idea of leading a good life. This definition of human development was made more explicit under the *Human Development Report of 2003* which said *"development must be woven around people, not people around development.*[107] After this, the idea of "sustainable development"[108] emerged, which extended the purview of human development beyond present generations and also enlarged the role of governments by bringing Civil Society's participation into various spheres of governance.[109]

The above paragraphs (features of Bangladesh's governance), as discussed above show that the government of the country is not running well. The government has failed to sustain the institutional arrangements and accountability relationships which yield good services. That means there is a gap between citizens and governments in terms of participation and public discussion. And because of this gap progress of the people and of the country, is not adequate. In 1990, when Bangladesh ended her military rule with the establishment of a parliamentary-democratic government, it had witnessed many socio-economic problems side by side with its political problems. Because Bangladesh is a poor country and natural disaster affected her badly, economic progress was and is an utmost priority. Therefore, the government of Bangladesh planned for poverty reduction and adopted measures for reduction of income poverty by establishing Civil Society Organisations (CSOs) and NGOs.

CSOs in Bangladesh have been shaped by the history of the country[110]. CSOs in Bangladesh claim to have a network of autonomous associations of rights-bearing and responsibility-laden citizens, created voluntarily to address common problems, advance shared interests and promote collective aspirations.[111] Like in other countries, CSO in Bangladesh work along with government and private institutions and carry on their work through NGOs. Therefore, in order to define Bangladesh's CSOs it is very important to discuss the role of NGOs. Nowadays, Bangladesh has more than 1000 NGOs, including advocacy groups and services organisations at national and local levels.[112] In Bangladesh, NGOs cover a wide-range of activities viz., micro-finance, health, educational services, social safety net programmes, agricultural extensions, social forestry, environmental protection, safe water and sanitations, disaster management and relief, legal and human rights educations, etc.[113] Though, it is true that by late 1980 the donors started funding the NGOs of Bangladesh, but it was only after the coming of democracy in 1990 that the NGO sector could build new alliances and develop new strategies in collaboration with CSO to influence and challenge the policies and practices of the government.[114]

The NGOs of Bangladesh do not face the constraints from various layers of government like the NGOs of India face. It may appear to be a plus point or a positive strength, but Bangladesh NGOs are not free from the clutches of government. The state laws define 'voluntary activity' as an activity which undertaken with partial or complete support from external sources, by any person or organisation to render voluntary services pertaining to agriculture, relief, missionary, educational, cultural, vocational, social welfare and other developmental activities in the country.[115] Though, the definition seems to cover almost all kinds of voluntary activities of NGOs yet in reality the state retains the right to include or exclude any activity as "voluntary". The NGOs are required to submit an annual report and the inspecting authority lies with the state. Therefore, neither the NGOs nor the CSOs are free from political party influences.[116] Thus, the nature of Bangladesh Civil Society is more national than global.[117] Hence, it can be said that the absence of a multi-layered government makes the Central government more powerful.

The above discussion shows that in Bangladesh local democracy/governance is not so strong vis-a-vis Central governance. The idea of local government was present in Bangladesh soon after independence. Some initiatives were taken in this direction of but because of long military rule the idea did not became a healthy reality as military rule used them (local governments) for their own purpose. It was in 1996 under the Awami League that local government got its present status.[118] The Awarni League constituted a Local Government Commission and came up with a report of Local Government Institutions. The Commission has recommended a four-tier local government structure including *Gram/Palli* (Village) *Parishad,* Union *Parishad, Thana/Upazila Parishad* and *Zila* (District) *Parishad.*[119] Each local category has their own functions but they faced many problems like elections are not regular and there is the dominance of political parties, etc. Therefore, though a Reform Commission was established by Awami League government but still there is long way to go.

After discussing the nature of government and governance in Bangladesh two things are quite clear. First there is a close relationship between a country's government and governance and secondly only democratic governance has the capacity to think beyond income by keeping human development as the primary focus. As it is the nature of government that decides the type of governance a country has, it is obvious that the ideologies of political parties, who either form the government and govern the country or sit in the opposition, matter much in providing governance. And the significance of democratic governance is considerable because it means the existence and enduring health of key institutions (presence of a system of representation, free and fair elections, presence of separation of powers an independent judiciary, a vibrant civil society and last but not the least, a free press and media)[120] which further empowers the people, the ultimate objective of a good government and of good governance.

Coming specifically to Bangladesh's nature of government and governance, it can be said that despite the presence of many features of democracy the result is not promising. The nature of democracy in Bangladesh is not fully participatory in nature and the political leaders do not follow the rules and regulation whether they are in opposition or in a ruling position, which makes the democracy more fragile and weak. Therefore, the solution to this problem is, firstly, that the political parties (ruling and opposition) must observe the democratic features not only for the welfare of the people, but more importantly for the sustainability of the democratic set-up. Secondly, the government must try to curb corruption[121] by incorporating institutional restraints, political accountability, effective public-private sector management and finally giving due respect to people's voice and participation. Otherwise Bangladesh would only be able to eradicate income poverty not human poverty. It is true that in general it is the aim of a government to remove income poverty that is to make those provisions which help in overcoming hunger but simultaneously the government must try to supplement and complement the income development efforts by human development, respecting human rights freedom and democracy. According to the HDR of 2006 Bangladesh's government had made a significant effort in removing income poverty but not with respect to removing human poverty.[122] That means Bangladesh is higher in comparative ranking of countries in terms of per capita income but lower in practicing democracy, giving freedom, options and choices to the people, despite its Constitutional commitment in this regard. Thus, it can be said that the government and governance of Bangladesh is participatory for politicians of political parties but not for the people of the country. This goes against the democratic sprit, which gave birth to Bangladesh.

References

1. Samir Kumar Das, 'Bangladesh: From Friendship to Partnership', in Changing Bangladesh: New Leap Forward, *World Focus*, Feb. 2010.
2. 'Constitution of Bangladesh', available in http://en.wikipedia.org/wiki/Constitution of Bangladesh (last accessed on *05/29/*10).
3. 'Bangladesh Government and Politics', available in http://countrystudies.us/bangladesh/82.htm (last accessed on 05/29/10).
4. Muhammed A. Tayyeb, 'Bangladesh: The Dilemmas of Independence', *Asian Affairs.* Vol. 5, No. 3, Jan-Feb, 1978, p. 169.
5. *Ibïd.,* pp. 169–170.
6. Mujib's rule withnessed murder, arson, robbery and smuggling. Corruption, nepotism, favouritism and bribery became the common order. Mujib's political opponents were put in prison or killed by the paramilitary group Jatiyo Rakkhi Bahini, *Ibid.,* p. 171.
7. *Ibid.,* p. 171.
8. Talukder Maniruzzaman, 'The Fall of Mujib Regime and Its Aftermath', *Asian Survey,* Vol. 16, No. 2, A Survey of Asia in *1975*, Part I, Feb., 1976, p. 120.

9. *Ibid.,* p. 120.

10. The Executive Committee of BKSAL (1) Sheikh Mujibur Rahman, (2) Sayed Nazrul lslam, (3) Mansoor AIi, (4) Khandakar Mushtaq Ahmed, (5) Abdul Hasnat Mohammad Kamruzzaman, (6) Abdul Malek Ukil, (7) Prof. Yusuf Ali, (8) Manoranjan Dhar, (9) Mohiuddin Ahmed, (10) Gazi Golam Mustafa, (11) Zillur Rahman, (12) Sheikh Fazlul Haq Moni, (13) Abdur Razzak.

    List of the Central Committee members of BKSAL (1) Sheikh Mujibur Rahman, (2) Sayed Nazrul lslam, (3) Mansoor Ali, (4) Abdul Malik Ukil, (5) Khandakar Mushtaq Ahmad, (6) A.H.M Kamaruzzaman, (7) Mahmudullah, (8) Abdus Samad Azad, (9) Yusuf Ali, (10) Fani Bhushan Majumder, (11) Dr Kamal Hussain, (12) Sohrab Hussain, (13) Abdul Mannan, (14) Abdur Rab Shemyabat, (15) Manoaranjan Dhar, (16) Abdul Matin, (17) Asaduzzanan, (18) Korban Ali, (19) Dr Azizul Rahman Mallik, (20) Dr. Mozzaffar Ahmed Choudhury, (21) Tofayel Ahmad, (22) Shah Moazzam Hossain, (23) Abdul Momen Talukder, (24) Dewan Farid Ganj, (25) Professor Nurul Islam Choudhry, (26) Taher uddin Thakur, (27) Moslemuddin Khan, (28) MD Nurul Islam Manju, (29) AKM Obaidur Rahman, (30) Dr Khitish Chandra Mandai, (31) Reazuddin Ahmad, (32) M. Baitullah, (33) Rahul Quddus (Secretary), (34) Zillur Rahman, (35) Mohiuddin Ahmad MP, (36) Sheikh Fazlul Haq Moin, (37) Abdur Razzaq, (38) Sheikh Shahidul Islam, (39) Anwar Choudhry, (40) Sajeda Choudhry, (41) Taslema Abed, (42) Abdur Rahim, (43) Abdul Awal, (44) Lutfur Rahman, (45) A.K. Muzibur Rahman, (46) Dr Mofiz Choudhry, (47) Dr Allauddin, (48) Dr Ahsanul Haq, (49) Raushan AIi, (50) Azizur Rahman Akkas, (51) Sheikh Abdul Aziz, (52) Salahuddin Yusuf, (53) Michale Shushil Adhikari, (54) Kazi Abdul Hakim, (55) Mollah Jalaluddin, (56) Shamsuddin Mollah, (57) Gaur Chandra Bala, (58) Gazi Ghulam Mustafa, (59) Shamsul Haq, (60) Shamsuzzoha, (61) Rafiqueuddin Bhuiya, (62) Syed Ahmad, (63) Shamsur Rahman Khan, (64) Nurul Haq,

(65) Kazi Zahurul Qayyum, (66) Capt. (Retd) Sujjat Ali, (67) M.R. Siddiqui, (68) M.A. Wahab, (69) Chittaranjan Sutar, (70) Sayeda Razia Banu, (71) Ataur Rahman Khan, (72) Khandakar Muhammad Illyas, (73) Mong Pru Saire, (74) Professor Muzzafar Ahmad, (75) Ataur Rahman, (76) Pir Habibur Rahman, (77) Sayeed Altaf Hussain, (78) Muhammad Farhad, (79) Motia Choudhury. (80) Hazi Danesh, (81) Taufiq Inam (Secretary), (82) Nurul Islam (Secretary), (83) Fayezuddin (Secretary), (84) Mahbubur Rahman (Secretary), (85) Abdul Khaleque, (86) Muzibul Haq (Secretary), (87) Abdur Rahim (Secretary), (88) Moinul Islam (Secretary), (89) Sayeeduzzaman (Secretary), (90) Anisuzzaman (Secretary), (91) Dr A. Sattar (Secretary), (92) M.A. Samad (Secretary), (93) Abu Tahir (Secretary), (94) Al Hossaini (Secretary), (95) Dr Tajul Hossain (Secretary), (96) Motiur Rahman. Chairman. TCB, (97) Maj. Gen. K.M. Safiullah, (98) Air Vice Marshal Khandakar, (99) Comodore M.H. Khan, (100) Maj. Gen. Khalilur Rahman, (101) A.K. Naziruddin, (102) Dr Abdul Matin Choudhury, (103) Dr Mazharul lslam, (104) Dr Sramul Haq, (105) ATM Syed Hossain, (106) Nurullslam, (107) Dr Nilima Ibrahim, (108) Dr Nurul Islam PG Hospital, (109) Obaidul Haq Eiditor Observer, (110) Anwar Hossain Manju Editor Ittefaq, (111) Mizanur Rahman BPI, (112) Manawarul Islam, (113) Brig. A.M.S. Nuruzzaman DG Jatiyo Rakki Bahini, (114) Kamruzzaman Teachers Association, (115) Dr Mazhar Ali Kadri.

In the same declaration five-sister organisations of BKSAL were also formed:

General Secretaries

1. Jatiyo Krishak League Fani Bhushan Majumdar;
2. Jatiyo Sramik League Professor. Yousuf Ali;
3. Jatiyo Mahila League Sajeda Choudhury;
4. Jatiyo Jubo League Tofayel Ahmed;
5. Jatiyo Chattra league Sheikh Shahidullslam. For more details see Azizul Karim's from Awami League to Baksal, available in http://www.sonarbangadesh.

com/Awami_ BAKSAL.html (last accessed on 05/23/10).

11. Parties which did not join BAKSAL were Jatiyo Samajtantric Dal, Purbo Bangladesh Sarbohara Party, Purbo Bangladesh Sammobadi Dal-Marxbadi-Leninbadi, East Pakistan Communist Party-Marxsist-Leninst, and Bangladesh Communist Party. Details in Talukder Maninuzzaman, *op. cit.,* pp. 120–121.
12. Muhammed A. Tayyeb, *op. cit.,* p. 173.
13. Talukder Maniruzzaman, *op. cit.,* p. 121.
14. Azizul Karim, "From Awami League to Baksal", available in http://www.sonarbangladcsh.com/Awami–BAKSAL.html (last accessed on *05/23/10).*
15. S.R. Chakravarty, *Bangladesh Under Mujib, Jia and Ershad: The Dilemma of a New Nation,* Har Anand Publication, New Delhi, 1995, pp. 8–10.
16. Talukder Maniruzzaaman, *op. cit.,* p. 122.
17. Muhammad Yeahia Akhter, *Electoral Corruption in Bangladesh,* Ashgate Publishing, England, 2001 pp. 55–56.
18. *Ibid.,* p. 56 and Talukder Maniruzzaman, *op. cit.,*pp. 122–123.
19. Talukder Maniruzzaman, *op. cit.,* p. 122.
20. See details in Muhammed A. Tayyeb, pp. 174–175.
21. *Ibid.,* pp. 175–176 and Talukder Maniruzzaman, *op. cit.,* pp. 123–124.
22. See more in Muhammad Yeahia Akhter, *op. cit.,* p. 56.
23. *Ibid.,* p. 56 and Talukder Maniruzzaman, *op. cit.*, pp. 125–127.
24. Coups and counter coups made the military of Bangladesh completely indisciplined and thus Zia had the fear that Abu Taher might organise another military coup. Therefore, he ordered his execution. Lawrence Lifschultz described the trial as a 'kangaroo trial'- which led to the expulsion of Taher from Bangladesh.

25. Zia was of the opinion that India's interference in the internal matters of Bangladesh led to the rise of destabilisation in Bangladesh. According to scholars that Zia had a belief that the reasons for the coups and counter-coups in Bangladesh was the result of India's pro-Mujib attituted. See more in R.L. Hardgrave, S.A. Kochanek, *India: Government and Politics in a Developing Nation,* Thomas Publishers, USA, 2008, p. 498.
26. Ziaur Rahman in his speech said:

    Now, I have been entrusted with enormous responsibility of serving as a head of the state. *Ins hallah*, this time also I shall completely devote myself to the service of the country and the nation with your support and cooperation. In this context, a referendum on the basis of direct universal adult franchise will be held on the so of next month to ascertain your confidence (in me). I hope you will help in building a stable and prosperous country expressing your opinion. See in *Muhammed A. Tayyeb, op. cit.,* p. 177.
27. *Ibid.,* p. 177.
28. See, Muhammad Yeahia Akhter, *op. cit.,* p. 57.
29. According to Zia through socio-economic development he could easily involve the masses in his political programme. This would further help him in influencing the people and he also believed that through rural development one could reach his goal, *Ibid.,* p. 57.
30. Zia recruited retired military persons, business people, retired civil servants, political leaders from leftist, rightist, liberal and Islamic organisations.
31. *Ibid.,* p. 58.
32. Muhammad Yeahia Akhter, *op. cit.,* p. 59.
33. 'Bangladesh—the Ershad period' available in http://www.monogabay.com/reference/country_studies/bangladesh/GOVERNMENT.html(last accessed on *06/02/10*).

34. 'Bangladesh—the Ershad' period available in http://www.monogabay.com/reference/country_studies/bangladesh/GOVERNMENT.html(last accessed on *06/02/10)*.
35. 'Bangladesh—the Ershad period' available in http://www.monogabay.com/reference/country_studies/bangladesh/GOVERNMENT.html(last accessed on *06/02/10)*
36. Muhammad Yeahia Akhter, *op. cit.,* p. 62.
37. Ershad had increased the status of military through promotions and pay increase, even in the police administration about 80 per cent of the SP's were military officials, *Ibid.,* p. 63.
38. 'New World Encyclopaedia', available in http://www.newworldencyclopedia.org/entry/Hossain *Mohammad_* Ershad (last accessed on 05/27/10).
39. 'New World Encyclopaedia', available in http://www.newworldencyclopedia.org/entry/Hossain Mohammad_Ershad (last accessed on *05/27/10)*.
40. Though, in the election Awami League and her 15-party alliance participated but after the election seven parties withdrew from it.
41. According to the opposition parties this move of Ershad led to the coming of armed forces in the polity of the country, that is the coming of military rule.
42. Awami League and BNP came together against the government and the meeting of opposition parties is known as "Siege of Dhaka". Government arrested the leaders of the opposing parties.
43. 'Bangladesh - Government: The Ershad Period', available in http://www.country-data.com/cgi- bin/gucry/r-1189.html (last accessed on 05/27/10).
44. Muhammad Yeahia Akhter, *op. cit.,* pp. 65–66.
45. Opposition parties jointly declared four points formula to address the situation:

1. Boycotting and resisting all elections under Ershad.
2. The resignation of Ershad and handover of power to NCG.
3. The restoration of credibility of electoral system and ensuring universal franchise by the NCG.
4. The transfer of power to a sovereign Parliament elected through free and fair elections conducted by the NCG.

46. 'Virtual Bangladesh: Biography Khaleda Zia', available in http://virtualbangladesh.com/biograohy/khaleda. html (last accessed on *03/11/10).*
47. 'Virtual Bangladesh: Biography Khaleda Zia', available in http://virtualbangladesh.com/biography/khaleda.html(last accessed on *03/11/10).*
48. Muhammad Yeahia Akhter, *op. cit.,* p. 67.
49. Under an NCG the incumbent prime minister and the cabinet would resign with the announcement of elections by the Election Commissioner followed by the dissolution of the Parliament by the President in accordance with the Constitution. The care-taker Prime Minister would act as the chief executive of the government under Article 55 of the Constitution, but would not be a candidate in the parliamentary elections. Therefore, the primary function of the NCG is to conduct a free and fair election in accordance with the Constitution. See more in Muhammad Yeahia Akhter, *op. cit.,* p. 68.
50. *Ibid.,* p. 69.
51. Inthe Magura-2 constituency during the election time the seat fell vacant due to the death of Awami League MP. Therefore, Awami League, BNP, and other parties wanted to occupy the seat. Election Commission tried hard to ensure free and fair election which resulted in the victory of BNP candidate. Thus, it was opposed by the opposition parties, *Ibid.,* pp. 60–62.
52. Details in 'Virtual Bangladesh: Biography' available in http://www.virtualbangladesh.com/biography/hasina (last accessed on *05129/10)* and also see more details in

'Bangladesh Awami League - Sheikh Hasina' available in http://www.albd.org/autoalbdindex. php?option =com_ 8task=view&id= 120&Hasina=44 (last accessed on 05/29/ 10).

53. Details in 'Virtual Bangladesh: Biography' available in http://www.virtualbangladesh.com/biography/hasina (last accessed on *05/29/10)*.
54. Sheikh Hasina established a house for poor people and she also ran an income generation programme in the rural areas called Asrayan.
55. In 1992, she launched a nationwide campaign to help the farmers and workers who were suffering from the neglectful attitude of the BNP government. Details in 'Virtual Bangladesh: Biography' available in http:// www.virtualbangladesh.com/biography/hasina (last accessed on *05/29/10)*.
56. India had erected a barrage on Ganga at Farakka, for navigable purposes. The necessity for this barrage arose because the principal current of Ganga, divides itself into two channels—one Padma flowing through Bangladesh and second Hooghly flowing through India. The problem is that in the lean period that is January to May, how would India get water for her various purposes. Though, many agreements were made but one or the other problem always emerged. But this clash was finally sorted out under Sheikh Hasina's government. See more in S.R. Chakravarty, *op. cit.,* pp. 124–128.
57. The area of Chittagong was suffering from a low-level of insurgency but after the Peace Accord the area was integrated into the mainstream of Bangladesh. See more in Details in 'Virtual Bangladesh: Biography' available in http://www.virtualbangladesh.com/biography/hasina (last accessed on 05/29/10).
58. Ali Riaz, 'Bangladesh in 2004: The Politics of Vengeance and The Erosion of Democracy', *Asian Survey,* Vol. 45, No. 1 (Jan-Feb, 2005), p. 112.

59. *Ibid.*, pp. 113–114.
60. *Ibid.*, p. 114
61. Rounaq Jahan, 'Bangladesh in 2003: The Vibrant Democracy or Destructive Politics?' *Asian Survey*, Vol. 44, No. 1 (Jan-Feb, 2004), pp. 59–60.
62. Ali Riaz, *op. cit.*, pp. 114–115.
63. *Ibid.*, pp. 115–116.
64. *Ibid.*, pp. 117–118.
65. Sheikh Hasina demanded the head of the care-taker government. President Iajuddin Ahmed should step down and a neutral NCG should be formed for conducting the election.
66. 'Sheikh Hasina', available in http://en.wikipedia.org/wiki/Sheikh_Hasina (last accessed on 08/29/10).
67. Sheikh Hasina', available in http://en.wikipedia.org/wiki/Sheikh_Hasina (last accessed on *08/29/10).*
68. As Sheikh Hasina said that charges against her was totally false and fake. Details in 'Virtual Bangladesh: Biography' available in http://www.virtualbangladesh.com/biography/hasina (last accessed on 08/29/10).
69. Sheikh Hasina was released because of her hearing impairment, eye problem and high blood pressure.
70. Smruti S. Pattanaik, 'New Dawn in Indo Bangladesh Relations?', in Changing Bangladesh: New Leap Forward, *World Focus,* Feb, 2010.
71. In January 2010, the Supreme Court of Bangladesh declared that Parliament does not possess any authority to suspend the Constitution and proclaim martial law.
72. Smruti S. Pattanaik, *op. cit.*,p. 43.
73. See Fardus Ara and Md. Mostafizur Rahman Khan's paper on 'Good Governance: Bangladesh Perspectives', *The Social Sciences* 1(2): 91-97, Rajshasi University, Bangladesh, 2006.
74. *Ibid.*, p. 91.

75. *Ibid.,* p. 92.
76. Rahman Sobhan, 'Structural Dimensions of Malgovernance in Bangladesh, *Economic and Political Weekly',* Vo1. 39, No. 36, 2004, pp. 4102–4103.
77. M.M. Hossain,paper on 'Democracy in Bangladesh: Problems and Prospects', Rajshahi University, Bangladesh.
78. Rahman Sobhan, *op. cit.,* p. 4103.
79. M. Serajul Islam, 'Is Bangladesh a Parliamentary Democracy?" available in http://www.theindependent-bd.com/details.php?nid=159914 (last accessed on 05/31/10).
80. In the 8th Parliament, the Awami League stayed out of the Parliament on the ground that BNP did not gave them the front seat, and the ruling party did not allow them to speak in the plenary sessions. The BNP government also used the same grounds when they are on the opposition side. See more http://www.theindependent-bd.comldetails.php?nid=159914 (last accessed on 05/31/10).
81. M. Harunur Rashid, 'Future of Parliamentary Democracy in Bangladesh', available In http://www.thedailystar.netinewDesign/news-details/php?nid= 114759 (last accessed on 05/31/10).
82. Rehman Sobhan, *op. cit.,*pp. 4103–4105.
83. *Ibid.,* p. 4105.
84. *Ibid.,* p. 4l05.
85. *Ibid.,* p. 4106.
86. When politicians become businessmen then they promote their private interests and neglect the public decisions and opinions. Thus, the division between the ruling party and opposition party is also invisible. See more details in *Ibid.,* p. 4106.
87. Fardaus Ara and Md. Mostafizur Rahman Khan, *op. cit.,* p. 94.
88. The allegation of partisanship arose because the ruling government of BNP refused to accept the services of 15

additional judges appointed under the Awami League. See Rounaq Jahan, *op. cit.,* pp. 58–59.

89. Muhammad Yeahia Akhter, *op. cit.,* p. 3.
90. Muhammad Yeahia Akhter, *op. cit.,* p. 112.
91. *Ibid.,* p. 112.
92. M.M. Hossain, *op. cit.,* p. 10.
93. BNP and Awami League united against the military rule of Ershad and demanded for the formation of NCG, but when they (BNP and Awami League) formed their government then they themselves were not ready for the formation of NCG.
94. M.M. Hossain, *op. cit.,* p. 13.
95. Ferdous Jahan, paper on 'Public Administration in Bangladesh', Centre for Governance Studies, BARC University, Dhaka, Bangladesh, 2006.
96. *Ibid.,* pp. 12–13
97. *Ibid.,* p. 14.
98. Rehman Sobhan, *op. cit.,*p. 4106.
99. BNP after becoming the ruling party in 1991 gave placement to party loyalist in important civil services and also manipulate the recruitment process. Therefore, when Awami League formed the government in 1996 then the senior civil servants started opposing the government.
100. The terms and conditions of government servant's rules 1975 are:
    1. No government servants shall be a member of or be associated with any political party, or any organisations affiliated to any political party, or shall take part, or assist to any manner, in any political activity in Bangladesh or abroad.
    2. No government servant shall permit any person dependent on him for maintenance or under his care and control to take part in or in anyway assist, any movement or activity which is, or tends directly or

indirectly to be subversive of government as by law established in Bangladesh.

3. No government servant shall canvass or otherwise interfere or use his influence in connection with or take part in any elections to a legislative body, whether in Bangladesh or elsewhere: Provided that government servant who is qualified to vote in such election may exercise his right to vote; but if he dose so, he shall give no indication of the manner in which he proposes to vote or has voted. See more details in Ferdous Jahan, *op. cit.,* p. 14.

101. *Ibid.,* p. 14.

102. 'Human development: health, education and social security', in *India: Democracy and Development,* Indira Gandhi National Open University, School of Social Science, New Delhi, 2004, p. 13.

103. According to the GNP approach the total (gross/net) produce of a country is converted into money value and when divided by the total population of the country gives per capita income. Human Capital Formation takes human beings as means not as ends. *Ibid.,* p. 11.

104. For example a poor man who cannot afford to send his children to school, but must send them to work in the fields, is lacking in human development. Similarly, a wealthy educated women whose gender excludes her from voting in election is also lacking human development. See details in Human Development Report 2002, p. 13.

105. 'Human Development: Health, Education and Social Security', in *India: Democracy and Development, op. cit.,* p. 15.

106. *Human Development Report 2002,* United Nations Development Programme (UNDP), New Delhi, 2002, p. 13.

107. Development should focus directly on the people, not just on nation-states. See details in Dr Arabinda Ghosh on Manual for Training of Trainers on Human

Development Part-I, Planning Commission—United Nations Development Programme (UNDP) sponsored project" *Strengthening State Plans for Human Development"*, Government of West Bengal, pp. 9–14.

108. Sustainable Development values human life. Therefore, it addresses both intra-generational and inter-generational equity to enable all generations, present and future, to make best use of their potentials. *Ibid.,* pp. 15–16.
109. Various parameters of Human Development are equity, job opportunities, access to productive assets, social spending, gender equality, population policy, good governance, etc., *Ibid.,* p. 21.
110. Anna. T. Schuramman and Simmin Mahmud, 'Civil Society, Health and Social Exclusion in Bangladesh, *Health Popular Nature,* Vol. 27, No. 4, 2009, p. 536.
111. 'BANGLAPEDIA : Civil Society', available in http://www.banglapedia.orgihttodocs/HTC0282.HTM (last accessed on *06/12/10).*
112. Anna. T. Schuramman and Simmin Mahmud, *op. cit.,* p. 537.
113. The Economics and Governance of Non-Governmental Organisations (NGO) in Bangladesh, 2005, Consultation Draft, by Poverty Reduction and Economic Management Sector Unit South Asian Region, p. 2.
114. *Ibid.,* p. 3.
115. M.M. Ahmed, 'The State, Laws and Non-Governmental Organisations (NGO's) in Bangladesh', *The International Non Profit Law,* Vol. 3, Issue 3, March 2001.
116. M.M. Ahmed, 'The State, Laws and Non-Governmental Organisations (NGO's) in Bangladesh', *The International Non Profit Law,* Vol. 3, Issue 3, March 2001.
117. Following are the problems suffers by Bangladesh NGO's:
    1. Undue interference and control of government.
    2. Political pressure and instability.

3. Lack of financial sustainability.
4. Religious conservatism, military dominance.
5. Lack of information and research, etc. See more details in Over View of Civil Society in NGO's of Bangladesh.

118. Local Government in Asia and Pacific: A Comparative Study, Country paper: Bangladesh, by United Nations Economic And Social Commission for Asia and Pacific.

119. All these tiers are concerned with rural or regional administration, while urban local governments remain outside the Commission's purview. The two major tiers of urban local government's, *Pourashava* (for smaller Municipalities) and City Corporation (for four of the largest cities) are in order. See more in Local Government in Asia and Pacific: A Comparative Study, Country paper: Bangladesh, by United Nations Economic and Social Commission for Asia and Pacific.

120. *Human Development Report 2002,* p. 4.

121. Factors which help in curbing corruptions:
    1. Independent and effective judiciary.
    2. Independent prosecution, enforcement.
    3. Healthy political competitions between political parties.
    4. Transparency in financing, public scrutiny.
    5. Partnership between private and public sectors.
    6. Freedom of information.
    7. Supporting the role of civil society and NGO's.
    8. Free media. See more details in *World Development Report 2004,* p. 197.

122. Dr Arabinda Ghosh on 'Manual For Training of Trainers on Human Development Part-I,' p. 24.

Conclusion

Now, from the above discussion, the two key words of my work are “secession” and “participatory governance”. The relationship between these two words is very complex and is situation specific. The urge for participatory governance need not always culminate into the demand for secession. Rather sometimes it culminates into a demand for human development. The terms majority and minority are the indicators for defining a country’s ethnic, social, political, cultural as well as economic distribution among its members or citizens. A minority group is that sociological group which does not constitute (numerically) a politically dominant voting group of the total population vis-a-vis the majority group of the total population of a given society, state and country.[1] But this is not the only way of mapping the minority group because lack of participation in day-to-day affairs of a country can also make a group a minority or subordinate group vis-a-vis the majority or dominant group. This gap, between the majority and minority, leads to a rise of inter-group conflict in a state. Therefore, the goal and aspirations of the majority and the minority group are not always complementary to each other. These two distinct groups see themselves as competing over zero-sum resources and have a conflictual attitude towards each other. And, the only way to overcome this conflictual attitude is if the groups view themselves as supportive to each other and have non zero-sum relations.[2]

According to Michael A. Hogg and Dominic Abrams, inter-group relations are not just about the attitude of the majority group towards the minority group rather it is more about the behaviour of the majority group towards the minority group. Because, generally the behaviour of the majority group towards the minority group is discriminatory and exclusionary, like the practice of in group favouritism, name-calling, verbal abuse, systematic violence and ultimately genocide.[3] Thus, there is a possibility that attitude does not always predict behaviour. Attitude is only about the mental view-point of a person, but on the contrary, behaviour is about human action. Though, attitude and behaviour are about consciousness of a person yet they are different in different experiences and circumstances. For example, inclusion of all democratic principles in the Constitution of Bangladesh is an indication of the positive attitude of the Bangladesh government and governance structure. But this did not (does not) change the behaviour of the majority towards the minority in Bangladesh. That means one can change his/her attitude towards accepting or negating a political, social or cultural phenomenon but when it comes to action (behaviour) then the situation for majority-minority relations might not change. Keeping this distinction in mind in the coming few pages. I would be focussing on the conditions of the minorities in the pre-secession period (East Pakistan) and in post-secession (Bangladesh).

The Awami League which primarily led the freedom struggle of Bangladesh grew out of the Bangla language movement and was thus based on Bengali nationalism and not on religion. Therefore, after independence Bangladesh emerged as a secular country with one dominant language group (Bengali) and with very few ethnic and religious minorities (Hindus, Buddhists and Christians). The new state of Bangladesh emerged as a secular polity with a constitutional embargo on religion in politics. The first Constitution passed on 4th November 1972, abolished: (a) all kinds of communalism; (b) political recognition of religion by the state; (c) exploitation of religion for political purposes; and (d) discrimination on religious grounds (Article 2 of the Bangladesh Constitution). The preamble of the Constitution declared secularism as one of the fundamental principles of state policy.[4] And under Article 3 Part 1, Bangla was adopted as the state language and Article 6 Part 1 declared that the citizens of Bangladesh were to be known as Bengali. The Bangladesh Constitution of 1972 in Article 9 defined Bengali nationalism as: *"The unity and solidarity of the Bangali nation, which deriving* its identity from its language and culture, attained sovereign and independent Bangladesh through a united and determined struggle in the war of independence, shall *be the basis of Bangali nationalism.*[5] Thus, it is clear that Bangladesh in its early phase believed in language identity (Bengali language) and not in religious identity (Muslim religion).

The creation of Bangladesh was rooted in the long suffering of people—especially the Bengali speaking people. Yet, if anyone asks a question, whether presently the minorities (specifically the Hindu minority) of Bangladesh[6] have the same rights and access to opportunities which the majority (Bengali Muslims) has, then unfortunately the answer would be no. Bangladesh in the recent past has witnessed an outburst of systematic attacks on Hindu minorities. For example, the Hindu dominated areas of Bangladesh like Barisal, Bhola, Khulna, Bogra and Brahmanbaria have been major targets, where Hindu houses have been destroyed and sacked, women raped and temples destroyed.[7] Because of this violence and unrest, more than 10,000 Hindu people fled from their homes to the Indian states of Tripura and West Bengal. This led to a rapid decline of the Hindu population in Bangladesh. The Hindu population in Bangladesh was 28 per cent in 1941, 22 per cent in 1951, 18.5 per cent in 1961, 13.5 per cent in 1974, 12.2 per cent in 1981 and 10.5 per cent in 1991. Thus, from 1961 to 1991 there was a sharp decrease in Hindu population.[8] Ethnic cleansing of minorities has become a common feature of Bangladesh, like the 2001 National Election resulted into forced migration of people from their "homeland of generations" for fear of their physical safety.[9]

Forceful conversion of Hindu minorities into Islam is also a major form of exploitation practiced in Bangladesh. Thus, it can be said that the language-based national identity on which Bangladesh was formed changed into a more religion oriented national identity, which again led to hostility between the majority Islamist and the Hindu minority. Thus, the secular character of Bangladesh Constitution rejecting all kinds of communalism, exploitation of religion for political purposes, as well as discrimination on religious grounds (this clause was adopted in 1974) was undermined. According to Article 41 of Bangladesh's Constitution, there is not only the guarantee of right to practice and promote religion, there is also the guarantee of individual right to refuse to practice a religion, or to be compelled to be educated in a religion other than one's own. Sections like 295, 296, 297, and 298 of the Penal Code deal with offences practiced against religious places or practices.[10] Therefore, despite the presence of these provisions in the Constitution of Bangladesh, there was firstly, the rise of an "Islamiyat politics of hegemony" taking the shape of "Islamic Nationalism" and this in turn became a hurdle for the minorities (especially Hindus). Sheikh Mujibur Rahman, in 1972 changed the nomenclature of the Enemy Properties Act (EPA) to that of a Vested Property Act (VPA), but discrimination continued against the minorities. VPA has been unjustly applied against both Hindu minorities and ethnic communities and made Hindus insecure because they have to prove ownership of long-held property.[11] Thus, Salem Samad says that "the spirit and essence of democracy is merely an illusion for the minorities as they always face the same pattern of discrimination and insecurity". Therefore, the suffering, loss and pain from which the Bengali Muslim minority of East Pakistan drew their commitment to the making of Bangladesh has not been translated into empathy for the suffering of other minorities. Even today, these minorities suffer from rape, murder, coercion, etc. Thus, the religious differences that were made into the main plank on which India was divided into two nations, and Pakistan was created for the Muslims, is again coming back as the central theme of confrontation in Bangladesh which however was created not on the basis of religious differences but on the issue of domination of an alien language over the mother tongue. This development indicates that the love of one's mother tongue which was a more important unifying factor than religious affinity is now evaporating as a social glue. Instead, religious affinity is becoming an increasingly important social binder in Bangladesh.

From the above discussion, it is clear that even after secession, the minorities are facing a variety of problems which otherwise should not have existed, had the secession had that inherent quality of overcoming the distinction of the majority from the minority. This is also an indication that despite Bangladesh being a Constitutional democracy, there is nonetheless a gap between Constitution and Constitutionalism. Despite this gap, it is observed that the condition of minorities of Bangladesh are better than the conditions of minorities in Pakistan. For example, though the genesis of the birth of Bangladesh was rooted in the independence of Pakistan in 1947, yet their political, social, economic and cultural trajectories were/are completely different from each other. The reasons behind the difference were mainly the dominance of one wing over another, which led to the demand for secession by the people of East Pakistan (see details in Chapter 2). Therefore, in the case of East Pakistan (now Bangladesh) the demand for secession was mainly based on the claim that there was a lack of participation in the political, social, economic and cultural life of United Pakistan by the people of East

Pakistan. The people of East Pakistan despite being the majority in terms of numbers faced the typical problems of "minorities". East Pakistanis were a numerical majority but a political-social-cultural-economical minority. In the case of Bangladesh the Bengali Muslims are in a majority, that is they are more than 90 per cent of the total population yet the present minorities of Bangladesh are not safe from assaults by sections of the majority. Hence, there is the demand for more participatory government and governance.

But there is also a sharp difference between pre secession Pakistan and today's Bangladesh. The minorities of Bangladesh, are not demanding secession like the minorities of United Pakistan had. Rather, the minorities of Bangladesh are demanding human rights. Therefore, the concern with which I have started this work, that is to analyse the relationship between the demands for secession and participatory governance, has becomes more important because we observe that lack of participatory governance does not always culminate into the demands for secession. However, that does not mean that participatory governance is less significant. Lack of participatory governance leads to many other tensions like demand for political autonomy, illegal immigration, border disputes. Given this historical reality, a central theoretical argument of this entire work is that a similar situation and cause lack of democratic rights (let alone participatory democracy) and persistence of ethnic discriminations do not necessarily lead to similar outcomes or forms of political tension or equivalent demands by oppressed groups. Context matters.

In Chapter 1, the term "secession" is regarded as a negative word because it brings the tag of "failed state" for the parent state. Therefore, states are always trying to avoid the stigma of being labelled a "failed state". Thus, the government of a state tries to have a system of governance where the demand for secession does not arise. And, the Constitutional way for overcoming this problem is the practice of democratic—participatory governance. This is the only type of governance which gives people a place in the affairs of a country and moreover the words "democracy" and "participation" act as a psychological support for the people of a country. Therefore, people (majority or minority) always make a demand for a more participatory model of democracy.

In the above paragraphs it was discussed that the demand for secession varies from context to context. In order to understand the context specific nature of the process of secession, we have taken the examples of both Pakistan and Bangladesh. Despite both the countries facing the problems of majority and minority tensions, their situation is not the same. The minorities of United Pakistan and of today's Pakistan are far more prone to demanding secession while the minorities of Bangladesh are not demanding secession. The reason for this difference is the presence of participatory democracy, however limited it may be, in Bangladesh and the absence of any stable democracy in today's Pakistan.

If we compare the developmental trajectories of Pakistan and Bangladesh, then we can say that both the countries share many things in common. For example, in the political realm both the countries have a very fragile practice of democracy and the military plays an active role. Despite this commonality, the difference is that Bangladesh has gone considerably further in its efforts to institutionalise stable civilian and democratic rule. Though, it is true that in Bangladesh the civilian government for a period of time did tilt towards religious extremist forces and towards the military. But it is equally true that Bangladesh has adopted various measures to overcome this earlier tilt. The major initiative in this respect came from the Supreme Court of Bangladesh on 29th July 2010, which nullified the 5th amendment of the Constitution and once again restored the secular principles of the Bangladesh Constitution.[12]

The above discussion shows that Pakistan and Bangladesh have a sharp difference in their political outlook, despite both having witnessed the changing combination of civilian and military rule. Bangladesh has travelled further on the democratic road but it still has some way to go considering its current identity crisis. That is "are we Bengalis first and Muslims second or Muslims first and Bengalis second.[13] The two major political parties of Bangladesh politics follow two distinct ideological paths.[14] This conflict between linguistic secular nationalism and a religious based nationalism generates a real uncertainty about the future. Using religion as a tool for gaining political legitimacy might lead to a stage where Hindu-Muslim clashes will become routine and discrimination against the minorities is further deepened. Even so secession would not be the answer for Bangladesh minorities. What guarantee is there that there would not be unjust discrimination against minorities in the seceding state? Fortunately, such a secession is not a serious prospect.

Thus, to conclude it can be said that secession is a double-edged weapon. Secession cannot be an end in itself except where it is both the only and the best democratic alternative. Short of such situations —as in Bangladesh— we need to have that type of governance which gives people more equal space by giving them much greater participation in every sphere of life. Democracy everywhere should be seen as unfinished business so that even where it exists in a stable proceduralist form, it needs to move further to becoming progressively more deliberative and participatory.

References

1. Minority Group' available at http://en.wikipedia.org/wiki/Minority_group (last accessed on *08/12/10*).
2. Michael A. Hogg, Dominic Abrams(ed.), *Inter-group Relations: Essential Readings,* Psychology Press, Philadelphia, 2001.
3. *Ibid.,* p. 7.

4. See 'Ethnic Cleansing in Bangladesh', available in http://www.hindujagruti.org/news/2328.html (last accessed on 06/10/10).
5. See 'Ethnic Cleansing in Bangladesh', available in http://www.hindujagruti.org/news/2328.html (last accessed on 06/10/10).
6. The major ethnic minorities of Bangladesh are Bhiharis, Chakma, Marrnas (Buddhist tribes) and *Stantal*, *Khasis*, *Garos, Kahjous*, etc. See David Levinson, Ethnic Groups World Wide: *A Ready Reference Handbook,* ORYX Press, Arizona, pp. 204–205.
7. Attack on Hindu Minorities', Voice of the AsiaPacific Human Rights Network 2001, available in http:/lwww.hrdc.net/sahrdc/hrfeaures/HRF48.htm (last accessed on 07/11/10).
8. Census Report of Bangladesh of 1991, available in Ethnic Cleansing in Bangladesh http://www.hintlujagruti.org/news/2328.html (last accessed on 06/10/10).
9. See Ethnic Cleansing in Bangladesh, available in http://www.hindujagruti.org/news/2328.html (last accessed on 06/10/10).
10. Salem Samad, 1998, 'State of Minorities in Bangladesh: From Secular to Islamic', available in http://www.mukto-moner.com/Articles/Saleem/Secular_to_islamic.htm (last accessed on 06/16/10).
11. Salem Samad, 1998, 'State of Minorities in Bangladesh: From Secular to Islamic', available in http://www.mukto-moner.com/Articles/Salcem/Secular_to_islamic.htm (last accessed on 06/16/10).
12. 'Restoring Bangladesh's Core Values', *The Hindu,* dated 08/02/10.
13. Lamia Karim paper presentation on 'In Search of Identity: The Rise of Political Islam and Bangladesh Nationalism' p. 2, available in http://web.unic.ca/-anp/Public/posish-pap/Karim.pdf (last accessed on *06/11/10).*
14. Awami League is the supporter of language-based identity but the contrary BNP is the supporter of religion-based identity.

Bibliography

Primary Sources

Charter of United Nations 1945, available in http://www.un.org/en/dpcuments/chater/index.shtml.

Constitution of Bangladesh 1972, available in *http://www*.1.umn./humanrts/research/bangladesh_constitution.pdf.

Handbook on Democracy Assessment, Kluwer Low International, 2002.

Human Development Report 2002, United Nations Development Programme (UNDP), Oxford University Press, New Delhi, 2002.

Manual for Training of Trainers on Human Development Part-I, prepared by Dr. Arabinda Ghose, Planning Commission–United Nations Development Programme (UNDP), sponsored project "Strengthening State Plans for Human Development", Government of West Bengal.

Promoting Democratic Governance, available in http://www.usaid.gov/jani/Chapter_1-Foreign_Aid_In_the National_Intersts.pdf.

Secondary Sources Books

Ahmed, Salahuddin, *Bangladesh Past and Present,* A.B.H. Publishers, New Delhi, 2004.

Akhter, Muhammad Yeahia, *Electoral Corruption in Bangladesh,* Ashgate Publishing, England, 2001.

Badruddin, Umar, *The Emergence of Bangladesh Vol. 1: Class Struggle in East Pakistan (1947–1958),* Oxford University Press, Karachi.

Bandyopadhya, Shekher, *From Plassey to Partition: A History of Modern India,* Orient Black Swan, India.

Bayefsky, Anne. F., *Self-determination in International Law:* Quebec and *Lessons Learned,* Kulwer Law International, Netherland, 2000.

Bhargav, Rajeev and Ashok Acharya, *Political Theory: An Introduction,* Pearson Publication, New Delhi, 2010.

Buchanan, Allen, *Secession: The Morality of Political Divorce Form Fort Sumter to Lithuania and Quebec,* Westview Press, 1991.

Catt, Helena, *Democracy in Practice,* Routledge, Oxon, 1999.

Chakravarty, S.R., *Bangladesh Under Mujib, Jia and Ershad: The Dilemma of a New Nation,* Har Anand Publication, New Delhi, 1995.

Chander, Prakash and Prem Arora, *Comparative Politics and International Relation,* Cosmos Bookhive, New Delhi, 1995.

Choudhury, Arshad, *Bangladesher Mukti Juddhho;* Bangla Academy, Dhaka, 1983.

Davis, Horace B, *Towards A Marxist Theory of Nationalism,* Monthly Review Press, New York, 1978.

Ganguly, Sumit, *Conflict Unending: India-Pakistan Tensions since* 1947, Oxford University Press, New Delhi, 2001.

Ghazali, Abdus Sattar, *Islamic Pakistan: Illusions and Reality,* National Book Club, 2006.

Goodin, Robert, P. Pettit and T. Pogge, *A Companion to Contemporary Political Philosophy,* Black Well Publishing, 2007.

Hasan, Mushirul, *India Partitioned: The Other Face of Freedom Vol. I,* Lotus Collection, New Delhi, 1995.

———— (ed.), *India's Partition: Process, Strategy and Mobilisation,* Oxford University Press, New Delhi, 200 I.

Islam, M. Rafiqul. *International Legal Implications: The Bangladesh Liberation Movement*, UPL, Dhaka, 1987.

Islam, Sirajul, *History of Bangladesh 1704-1971, Cultural History,* Asiatic Society of Bangladesh, Dhaka, 1992.

Islam, Sirajul, *History of Bangladesh 1704-1971, Economic History,* Asiatic Society of Bangladesh, Dhaka, 1992.

__________, *History of Bangladesh: 1704-1971, Political History,* Asiatic Society of Bangladesh, Dhaka, 1992.

Jahan, Rounaq, *Bangladesh Promise and Performance.* UPOL, Dhaka, 2004.

Kohen, M.G., *Secession: International Law Perspectives,* Cambridge University Press, 2006.

Lalonde, Suzanne, *Determining Boundaries in Conflicted World: The Role of UTI-possibilities,* McGill-Queen's University Press, Canada, 2002.

Lifschultz, Lawrence, *Bangladesh: The Unfinished Revolution.* Zed Press, London, 1979.

Lowy, Michael, *Fatherland or Mother Earth? Essay on National Question, 1998,* Pluto Press, London.

Mckinnon, Catriona, *Issues in Political Theory,* Oxford University Press, New York, 2008.

Pavkovic, Aleksandar and Peter Radan, *Creating New States: Theory and Practice of Secession*, Ashgate Publishing Limited, England, 2007.

__________, *On The Way To Statehood: Secession and Globalisation,* Ashgate Publishing Limited, England, 2007.

Sen, Amartya, *Identity* and *Violence: The Illusion of Destiny,* Penguin Group, New York, 2006.

Shaw, M.N., *International Law,* Cambridge University Press, 2005.

Sisson, Richard and Leo. E. Rose, *War and Secession: Pakistan. India and Bangladesh, University of California Publishing,* England, 1990.

Vanaik, Achin, *India in a Changing World, Orient Longman,* India, 1995.

Wellman, Christopher Heath, *A Theory of Secession: The Case for Political Self-determination,* Cambridge University Press, New York, 2005.

Articles

Ahmed, M.M, 'The State, Laws and Non-Governmental Organisations (NGO's) in Bangladesh'. *The International Non-Profit Law,* Vol. 3, Issue 3, March 2001.

Amato, Paul D., 'The Meaning of Marxism : Marxist and the Right to Self-determination'. June 21, 2002, available in http://socialistworker.org/2002-2/411141109 Self Detennination.shtml.

Ara, Furdos and Md. Mostafizur Rahman Khan's paper on 'Good Governance' Bangladesh Perspectives', *The Social Sciences* 1 (2): 91–97, 2006, Rajshasi University, Bangladesh.

Asadullah, M. Niaz, *'Educational Disparities in Pakistan: 1947–* 1971 (presentation paper of UK Economic and Social History Conference), 2004.

Buchanan, Allen, 'Towards a Theory of Secession', *Ethics,* Vol. 101, No. 2, 1991.

————, 'Theories of Secession', *Philosophy and Public Affairs,* Vol. 6, No. 1, 1997.

Chambers, Simone, 'Deliberative Democratic Theory', *Annual Review of Political Science, 2003.*

Choudhury, G.W., 'Bangladesh Why it Happened?' *International Affairs,* Vol. 48, No. 2, April 1972.

Chris Harman, 'The Return of the National Question', *International Socialism 56,* Autumn 1992.

Das, Samir Kumar,' Bangladesh: From Friendship to Partnership', in Changing Bangladesh: New Leap Forward, *World Focus*, Feb. 2010.

Jahan, Ferdous, paper on 'Public Administration in Bangladesh', Centre for Governance Studies, BARC University, Dhaka, Bangladesh, 2006.

Jahan, Rounaq, 'Bangladesh in 2003: The Vibrant Democracy or Destructive Politics'?', *Asian Survey,* Vo1. 44, No. 1, Jan.-Feb. 2004.

Kreptual, Anderi, 'The Constitutional Right to Secession in Political Theory And History', *Journal of Libertarian Studies,* Vol. 17, No. 4, Fall 2003.

Landy, Sy, 'Self-determination and Military Defence: The Marxist Method', *Proletarian Revolution* 59, *Summer* 1999 (Transcribed, Edited and Formated by Damon Maxwell and David Walters in 2008 for the Encyclopaedia of Trotskyism, available in http://www.marxist.org/history/etol/writers/landy/1999/xx/military.htm.

Lenin on 'What is Meant by Self-determination of Nations'?', available in http://www.marxist.org/archive/Lenin/works/1914/self-det/ch01.htm.

Lewis, Tom, 'Marxism and Nationalism', *International Socialist Review,* Issue 13, Aug-Sep. 2000, available in http://www.isreview.org/issues/13/Marxism_nationalism_part1.shtml.

London, Scott, "Tele-democracy vs. Deliberative Democracy: A Comparative Look at Two Models of Public Talk', *Journal of Interpersonal Computing and Technology,* Vol 3, No 2, April 1995.

Maniruzzarnan, Talukder, 'The Fall of Mujib Regime and its Aftermath', *Asian Survey.*Vol. 16, No. 2, A Survey of Asia in 1975, Part - II, Feb. 1976.

McNally, David, 'Marxism, Nationalism and National Struggles Today' (A *Discussion Document for New Socialist Group,* 1996, available In *http://www*.newsocialist.org/index.php?option=com content&view=articl e&id= 1 488Itemid=75.

Munck, Ronnie, 'Otto Bauer: Towards A Marxist Theory of Nationalism', *Capital and Class,* 1985, Vol. 9 No. I.

Nanda, V.P. 'Self-determination Under International Law: Validity of Claims of Secede' 13 Case Western Reserve, *Journal of International Law,* 1981.

Pattanaik, Smruti S., 'New Dawn in Indo-Bangladesh Relations?', in Changing Bangladesh: New Leap Forward, *World Focus.* Feb., 2010.

Pavkovic, Aleksandar and Peter Radan, 'In Pursuit of Sovereignty and Self-determination: Peoples, States and Secession in the International Order'. *Macquire Law Journal,* Vol. 3, 2003.

Riaz, Ali, 'Bangladesh in 2004: The Politics of Vengeance and The Erosion of Democracy', *Asian Survey,* Vol. 45, No.1, Jan-Feb, 2005.

Rudi Gurazin, 'Is Humanitarian Military Intervention in the Affairs of Another State Ever Justified?'*Global Political Security and International Studies Middlesex University,* 2008.

Schuramman, Anna. T and Simmin Mahmud, 'Civil Society, Health and Social Exclusion in Bangladesh, *Health Popular Nature,* Vo1. 27, No. 4, 2009.

Sobhan, Rahman, 'Structural Dimensions of Mal-governance in Bangladesh, *Economic and Political Weekly',* Vol. 39, No. 36, 2004.

Tayyeb, Muhammed A., 'Bangladesh: The Dilemmas of Independence', *Asian Affairs,* Vol. 5, No. 3, Jan.-Feb., 1978.

Yates, Stevens, 'When is Political Divorce Justified?' in David Gordon (ed.), *Secession, State and Liberty,* Transaction Publishers, New Jersey.

Newspapers and Journals

The Hindu
The Statesman
Asian Affairs
Asian Survey
Capital and *Class*
Economic and Political Weekly
International Affairs
Journal of International Law
Journal of Libertarian Studies
Libertarian Studies
Philosophy and Public Affairs
World Focus

Index

A

Abdus Sattar
  Regime, 101
Abu Taher
  coups, 123
  expulsion, 123
Agartala Conspiracy Case, 88
Attitude and Behaviour, 136
August 15 Coup of 1975, 97
Autonomy, 15
Awami League
  and BNP Alliance, 103
Awami League, 136
  victory 2008, 108
  -BNP Coalition, 125
Ayub Khan
  Pakistan Under, 71

B

Bangladesh
  birth of, 55
  ..genesis, 55
  nature/governance, 136
  creation, 137
  refugees in India, 74
  sectors division/command, 74
  problems, 96
  Declaration of Independence, 73
  Secession, 21
  War declaration, 90
  ..sectors, 91
  Government structure, 95
Bangladesh Krishak Shramuk
  Awami League, (BKSAL)
  impact, 98
  abolishment, 99
  Executive Committee, 121
  Central Committee, 121
  Five Sister organisations, 122
Bangladesh Nationalist Party
  (BNP), 101
  as ruling party, 105
  third tenure, 106
  problems in, 107
Bauer, Otto
  interpretation of nation, 37
  on culture-role, 37
Bengal Partition, 57
  ..Curzon on, 57
  ..Division at Partition, 62
Bengal
  under British, 58

history, 57
independant province, 57
Culture protection, 68
Language identity, 68
issue, 69
demand, 69
Bhutto, Z.A., 71
Bi-Party System, 109
Black Day Bangladesh, 72
Bolshevik Revolution, 40
Breakdown Plan, 85
Breaking/Making
of States
.. reasons, 19
Buchanan, Allen
on Secession, 29, 32-34
Bureucratic Structure-Bangladesh
problems, 114

C

Cabinet Mission Plan, 85
Categorical identities, 16
Civil-Military Relations
East-West Pakistan, 71
Civil Society Organisations, 117
Communalism, 82
Constitution Amendment
Bangladesh
..1975, 98
..1977, 101
Constitution Bangladesh, 96, 137
Constitutional Amendments
under Khaleda Zia, 105
Conversions, 138
Corruption
factors curbing, 133
Counry's Governance
- concept, 108
aspects, 108-109
Coups in Bangladesh, 100
Criminilisation of politics, 111
Bangladesh, 111
Cultural National Autonomy
- Bauer, 37
Curzon Lord
on Bengal, 58
on Partition, 82

D

Davis Horace B.,
Book
-*Towards a Marxist Theory of Nationalism*, 38
Deliberative Democracy, 45
Democracy
role, 43
forms, 44
Democracy in Bangladesh, 119
Direct Democracy, 44-45
Divide and Rule Policy, 58, 60

E

East Pakistan
Communist Party, 74
East Pakistanis
exploitation, 72-73
East-West Pakistan
linkage, 63
disparities, 96
- factors, 63-64
economic disparities, 67

..reasons, 68
educational Disparities, 70
Civil - Military Relations, 71
separation/ secession, 59
Economic Disparities
East-West Pakistan, 67
Electoral Crisis/Corruption, 112-13
Emergency Declaration 1974, 98
Ershad, Hussain
Muhammad, Gen.
regime, 102
objectives, 102
demand for
resignation, 104-105
European Countries
in India
..Reasons for coming, 57

F

Failed State, 27
Farakka Barrage, 127

G

GOI Act 1909, 59
Good Governance, 20
Governance
-Bangladesh, 115
Government and Governance, 119
Govt. serevants
rules 1975
..terms, 130-31

H

Hindu Population
-Bangladesh, 137
Hindu-Muslim Divide, 59-60
Hindutva, 61
Human Development
Index (HDI), 116
Human Development, 115
Human Rights
categories, 93

I

India
intervention in Bangladesh
Justification of, 78-79
India in a Changing
World, 40-41
-Achin Vanaik, 40-41
India interference, 124
India-Pakistan
War (1971), 75
US/Soviet role, 75
surrender, 76
Indo-USSR Peace
Treaty, 75
Islamic Nationalism, 138

J

Jinnah vision, 72
Judiciary status, 112
Just War Theory, 79

K

Khaleda Zia
as PM, 105

L

Lahore Declaration, 61
Law Enforcement, 111
Leftists role
in Bangla War, 74

Lenin
on Self Determination, 36
Theory of nationalism, 39-40
..reformulation, 40
Liberation War (Bangladesh)
India role, 73-74
Local Democracy/Governance, 118
Local Government Institutions, 118
Luxemburg, Rosa
on Autonomy, 38
on Self determination, 38
on nation, 39

M

Martial Law
- Pakistan-1958, 71
Marxist Approach
to Nationalism, 34
to right to self determination, 35
Mastaans, 112
Military Intervention
viewpoints, 78
humanitarian angle, 78
Military Rule
end, 105
Minorities
problems of, 139
Mountbatten Plan, 86
Morley Minto
Reform 1909, 58, 82-83
Mountbatten Plan, 61-62
Movement for
Restoration of Peace, 103
Mukti Bahini, 90
training/camps, 74-75
..India role, 74
.. strategies adopted, 91
Mushirul Hasan, 84
Mushtaq Ahmed
President, 99
Muslim League
formation, 59
growth, 61
Muslim Nationhood
idea of, 60
Mutiny 1857, 82

N

Nation
view on, 39
Stalin on, 39
National identities, 17
Nationalism, 16, 62
meaning, 17
Marxist Approach to, 35, 38
NCG formation, 113
NGOs Bangladesh, 117
problems, 132-33
Non-Party Caretaker
Government (NCG), 105
proposal for, 105

O

One Unit Bill
East-West Pakistan, 89
Operation Searchlight, 73

P

Pakistan
  formation basis, 83-84
  Government model/system, 63
  political power, 64
  Parliamentary Democracy
    ..failure, 87
Pakistan-Bangladesh
  commonalities, 141
Parity of Representation
  East-West Pakistan, 88
Parliamentary Elections
  under Ershad, 104
    ..boycott, 104
  Feb. 1996, 106
  June 1991, 106
Parliamentary democracy
  Bangladesh, 110
    ..features, 110
Participatory Democracy, 46-47
Participatry Governance
  concept, 41
Partition of Bengal, 82
  news, 83
Plan Balkan, 86
Political freedom
  indicators, 43-44
Political Liberalism/
  freedom, 15
Politicians
  East/West Pakistan, 87
Presedential Form
  of Government, 98
Procedural Democracy, 45
Proletarian Internationalism, 37

R

Recognition to
  Bangladesh, 80-81
Referendum 1985, 103
Remedial Right Theory, 80
Representative Democracy, 45
Right to Practice
  and promote Religion, 138
Right to Self
  Determination, 76
  theory, 77
Russian Social
  Democratic Party (RSDLP)
    Congress-1903,
    ..issues, 36
    ..Article 9, 36

S

Savarkar's Doctrine
  -Hindutva, 61
Secession, 15, 19, 142
  Movements, 18
  ..Reasons, 20
  meaning, 26
    definition, 27
    properties, 27
  genesis, 29
  concept, 28
  stigma, 140
    historical egs, 28
  and Participatory
    Governance, 135
Secular character, 138

Self-determination,15, 17
and secession, 30
..Marxist version, 34-35
..right to, 30
..in UN Charter, 31
..Lenin on, 36
Sheikh Hasina
works, 127
as PM, 106, 108
extortion charges, 107
arrest, 107
release, 128
charges against, 128
Sheikh Mujibur Rehman
Government, 96
as President, 98
coup, 99
failure, 99
hatred, 98
Sheikh Mujibur Rehman's
declaration of Independence, 73
Six Point Programme, 65
demand of Federal Government, 65
victory in elections, 66
Jail/implication, 66, 73
Shekh Hasina/Khaleda Zia
imprisonment, 103
Six Point Programme
East Pakistan reaction on, 65-66
Soviet role
in Indo-Pak War, 75
Stalin
on Nation, 39
Sustainable Development, 116, 132
Syed Nazrul Islam, 72

T

Task Force 74-US, 92
Territory (nature), 27
Theory and Practice
-concept, 25
Tiers of Local Governments, 133
Trotsky
view on nation concept, 39
Two Nation Theory
-Jinnah, 61

U

UN Charter on Human Rights, 77
Support to east Pakistan, 80
on Right to Interferences in Internal Matters, 78
US
Pakistan support
reasons, 92
role in Indo-Pak War, 75

V

Vested Property
Act (VPA), 138
Voluntary Activity, 117

Y

Yahya Khan rule, 70

Z

Zia ur Rahman
Maj. Gen.
fall and rise, 100
Referendum, 10
changes under, 101
assassination, 101